# The Ultimate Comma Guide

*A Reference and a Textbook*

**Gentry Sutton**

Cover image © Shutterstock, Inc.

www.kendallhunt.com
*Send all inquiries to*:
4050 Westmark Drive
Dubuque, IA 52004-1840

Copyright © 2015 by Kendall Hunt Publishing Company

ISBN 978-1-5249-5562-5

All rights reserved. No part of this publication may be reproduced, stored in a retrieval system, or transmitted, in any form or by any means, electronic, mechanical, photocopying, recording, or otherwise, without the prior written permission of the copyright owner.

Published in the United States of America

# Table of Contents

Introduction ............................................................................. vii

Chapter 1: Foundational Vocabulary for Comma Instruction ............ 1
    1.A: Parts of Speech ................................................................. 1
        Nouns ................................................................................ 1
        Verbs ................................................................................. 3
        Pronouns ........................................................................... 5
        Adjectives .......................................................................... 7
        Adverbs ............................................................................. 9
        Prepositions ..................................................................... 12
        Conjunctions ................................................................... 14
        Interjections .................................................................... 15
    1.B: Subjects and Predicates ................................................... 16
    1.C: Predicate Complements .................................................. 19

Chapter 2: Independent and Dependent Clauses ............................ 23
    2.A: Clauses vs. Phrases ......................................................... 23
    2.B: Independent and Dependent Clauses ............................... 24

Chapter 3: Introductory Elements ................................................. 41
    3.A: Adverbs ......................................................................... 41
    3.B: Transitional Expressions ................................................. 44
    3.C: Participles ...................................................................... 46
    3.D: Interjections .................................................................. 48
    3.E: Phrases .......................................................................... 49
        Prepositional Phrases ....................................................... 49
        Participial Phrases ........................................................... 53
        Infinitive Phrases ............................................................. 55
        Absolute Phrases ............................................................. 57

Chapter 4: Mid-Sentence and End-of-Sentence Elements ................ 59
    4.A: Nonrestrictive Elements ................................................. 59
    4.B: Parenthetical Expressions ............................................... 64
    4.C: Conjunctive Adverbs and Other Transitional Expressions .... 66

## Table of Contents

 4.D: Contrasting Elements ................................................................. 69

Chapter 5: Standard Serial Items and Coordinate Adjectives ............... 71
 5.A: Standard Serial Items ................................................................ 71
 5.B: Coordinate Adjectives ............................................................... 73

Chapter 6: Quotations and Dialogue, Direct Address, and Tag Questions ................................................................................................. 77
 6.A: Quotations and Dialogue ......................................................... 77
  Quotations That Follow Explanatory Information and End a Sentence ............................................................................................ 78
  Quotations That Begin a Sentence and Are Followed by Explanatory Information .................................................................. 81
  Quotations That Occur in the Middle of Sentence .................... 82
  Quotations That Are Broken by Explanatory Information ...... 84
 6.B: Direct Address ........................................................................... 85
 6.C: Tag Questions ............................................................................. 86

Chapter 7: Dates, Addresses and City/State Locations, Titles and Designations, Numbers, and Correspondence ....................................... 89
 7.A: Dates ............................................................................................ 89
 7.B: Addresses and City/State Locations ....................................... 91
  Cities and States ............................................................................ 91
  Full Addresses ............................................................................... 92
 7.C: Titles and Designations ............................................................. 93
 7.D: Numbers ..................................................................................... 94
  Regular Numerals ......................................................................... 94
  Measurements, Parts, and Categories ....................................... 95
 7.E: Correspondence .......................................................................... 96

Chapter 8: Difficult Cases and Rules Less Frequently Needed ............ 97
 8.A: Serial Items with Internal Commas ........................................ 97
 8.B: Placement of Commas When They Are Used with Parentheses ................................................................................ 99
 8.C: "The More," "The Better," "The Greater," and Similar Phrases ................................................................................. 100
 8.D: Internal Monologue ................................................................. 101

Table of Contents

    Internal Monologue That Follows Explanatory Information and Ends a Sentence ............................................................... 101
    Internal Monologue That Begins a Sentence and Is Followed by Explanatory Information ....................................... 103
    Internal Monologue That Occurs in the Middle of a Sentence .................................................................................. 104
    Internal Monologue That Is Divided by Explanatory Information ............................................................................... 105
  8.E: Questions Referred to within Sentences ................................... 106
  8.F: "Not Only...But Also..." Sentence Constructions .................... 107
  8.G: Homonyms That Appear Beside Each Other ............................ 108
  8.H: Commas to Indicate Omission ................................................... 109
  8.I: Sentences Containing Two Introductory Elements ................... 111

Chapter 9: Common Comma Misuses ....................................................... 115
  9.A: The Comma Splice ....................................................................... 115
  9.B: Compound Elements .................................................................... 117
  9.C: Comma Misuse with Subordinating Conjunctions .................. 120
  9.D: Dates, Holidays, and Seasons ..................................................... 120
  9.E: Family Titles .................................................................................. 121
  9.F: Elements Not Usually Separated by Commas .......................... 122
    Subjects and Their Verbs .............................................................. 122
    Action Verbs and Their Complements ....................................... 123
    Linking Verbs and Their Complements ..................................... 124
    Prepositions and Their Objects .................................................... 125
    Prepositional Phrases That Follow Other Major Sentence Elements .......................................................................................... 126
  9.G: First and Last Items in a Series ................................................... 128
  9.H: First and Last Coordinate Adjectives ........................................ 129

Appendix: List of Comma Rules with Rule Examples ........................... 131

Index of Subjects ........................................................................................ 155

# Introduction

The comma is a small punctuation mark, but it has some big responsibilities in the English language. It can affect not only the *flow* of a written thought but also the *meaning* of a sentence. The comma is so important, in fact, that it has some type of relationship to many of the terms and concepts of English grammar.

The comma's relationship to other English-language issues is at the heart of this book. As a professional editor and a teacher of English, I have observed that the vast majority of sentence-level writing mistakes made by students and professionals alike are related in some manner to comma usage. Writers misuse commas or neglect to use them in part because they do not understand rules and concepts that are indirectly related to comma usage. For example, the first rule of this book states that "a sentence comprised of two independent clauses should be joined by both a comma and a coordinating conjunction, and the comma should be placed before the conjunction." A writer who does not know the definition of an independent clause or a coordinating conjunction will probably fail to employ this rule consistently. Conversely, a writer who *does* understand how to use commas will likely have a solid grasp of other important grammatical concepts and, consequently, be an above-average writer, at least at the sentence level. Because so many writing mistakes are related to comma usage (or misuse), I set out to write *The Ultimate Comma Guide* because I believe that people can significantly improve their command of the written sentence by mastering comma usage.

For many years, comma instruction has revolved around six to nine major rules. (The number has depended on textbook authors' perspectives and how they categorized certain comma-related issues.) As I began to write this book, I questioned the effectiveness of comma instruction that is expressed in only six to nine general rules instead of in many more concrete, detailed rules. Consider, for example, textbook authors' traditional instruction about using commas to "set off" transitional words and expressions such as *however*. As an editor, I have encountered hundreds of documents in which authors have "set

## Introduction

off" the transition/conjunctive adverb *however* when they used it in the middle of a sentence, but they "set it off" on only one side. When *however* is used as a transitional expression in the middle of a sentence and it is not joining complete thoughts, it always requires commas on both sides.

- *Incorrect*: Jillian performed well at the recital. Her sister however, missed a few notes.
- *Correct*: Jillian performed well at the recital. Her sister, however, missed a few notes.

As I reviewed textbooks containing comma instruction and encountered such phrases as "set off," I started to wonder if mistakes such as the one described above were the results of flawed instruction. Perhaps authors who use commas on just one side of *however* are, in their minds, "setting off" the word, believing that "setting off" simply refers to using only one comma.

Consider also the traditional rule of placing commas after introductory elements. While most textbooks provide examples of the various types of introductory elements, the examples are seldom exhaustive. Moreover, textbooks often list adverbs as a type of introductory element, but they sometimes fail to indicate that adverbs used as introductory elements must meet certain criteria before they require a comma. For example, while many adverbs require a comma when they are used at the beginning of a sentence, as in the first example below, an adverb of direction does not usually require a comma, even if it begins a sentence. Moreover, sentence-beginning adverbs that require commas usually must describe verbs—not adjectives or other adverbs. However, these exceptions and criteria are not generally specified in textbooks.

- *Cautiously*, the police officer approached the driver of the stolen car. (*Cautiously* describes the verb *approached*.)
- *Westward* the pioneers went in search of gold. (*Westward* is an adverb of direction and therefore does not require a comma.)

# Introduction

- *Beautifully* dressed celebrities mingled at the ball. (*Beautifully* describes the adjective *dressed*, not a verb, so it does not require a comma.)

Because I have, as an editor and a teacher, so often seen comma-related mistakes that I believe may be the result of imprecise language in the usual wording of comma rules, I have endeavored to state rules more explicitly than they are usually stated in handbooks. In regard to introductory elements, for example, readers will find an entire chapter that contains eleven detailed rules, not just one general rule that "a comma should follow an introductory element."

As I began to expand the traditional six to nine comma rules into an eventual seventy-one, I realized that I was composing an authoritative reference for professional editors and writers. By turning six to nine general (and sometimes vague) principles into seventy-one well-defined rules, I hope that I have created a reference that students, professional writers, and editors will find helpful. While comma usage in some situations will always be governed by authorial or editorial preference, and while I have called attention to the instances in which such preference may supersede a "rule," I have tried to give editors and authors a tool with which they can eliminate much guesswork related to comma usage.

Not far into the book, I realized that I was writing something that the general public could use as well. Many people have questions about comma usage and would like an easy-to-use tool to improve their writing at the sentence level. It is my hope that this books meets that need.

Writing *The Ultimate Comma Guide* was a labor of love and passion. As a writing instructor, I know firsthand that writing instruction for the past two or three decades has focused on whole-essay instruction at the expense of more basic instruction. In the college classroom, I see a number of students who have a solid understanding of the five-paragraph essay but struggle to write mechanically correct sentences. Unfortunately, a well-structured piece of writing is ineffectual in both the classroom and in the workplace if it is riddled with mistakes at the sentence level.

Introduction

While I understand that basic writing instruction cannot be simplified to comma instruction (issues such as subject-verb agreement, tense consistency, proper pronoun usage, and syntax are certainly issues with which even college students struggle), I believe that *The Ultimate Comma Guide* can be used not only as a reference but also as a textbook alongside more traditional texts. After all, to master comma usage, students must understand fundamental concepts such as the difference between a clause and a phrase, the difference between an independent clause and a dependent clause, the difference between a restrictive element and a nonrestrictive element, and much more. I have used content from *The Ultimate Comma Guide* in my own writing courses, including College Composition I, English Grammar, and Foundations of Writing and Editing. Some students have expressed appreciation for receiving sentence-level instruction, acknowledging that they failed to practice many sentence-level concepts enough at lower levels in the educational system.

*The Ultimate Comma Guide* may also serve as a great text for students at both the master's and doctoral levels as they prepare to write theses and dissertations. As a former academic editor, I am all too aware that even doctoral students struggle with sentence-level mechanics. *The Ultimate Comma Guide* may help candidates for graduate degrees avoid a lot of laborious editorial work when they reach the writing stage of their programs.

Some of the rules found in *The Ultimate Comma Guide* require an understanding of basic grammatical terminology and concepts. Therefore, the book contains instruction to ensure that students master that terminology and those concepts before they attempt to complete the exercises that are more directly related to comma usage. In fact, the entire first chapter is a review of the most basic grammatical terms and concepts.

The entire book may or may not be appropriate for any given classroom. In my College Composition I course, I have used only content from chapters 2–6 and chapter 9—and then only parts of certain chapters. Chapters 7 and 8 contain rules that are less frequently needed. The information presented in these chapters may not be important enough to take the place of instruction about other topics that should be covered in a composition course, but these chapters may

## Introduction

serve as valuable secondary resources for students. In my English Grammar course, I have used the entire text during the last one-fourth of the semester as a way to help students review and apply important lessons learned earlier in the semester.

Not everyone will agree with my approach to this book. Some people will find the specificity of the seventy-one-rule approach unnecessarily laborious and pedantic. Such people likely have a good enough command of grammatical concepts and of the English language that the traditional six-to-nine, general-rule approach is sufficient for them. To be sure, some rules, particularly some in chapters 6 and 8, are admittedly rather dense in their specificity. I maintain that these rules may help editors and students for whom general rules are insufficient, and I have erred on the side of precision at the expense of concise, memorize-able rules.

Some seasoned writers and editors may also disagree with a few of the rules themselves. Most of the rules that are perhaps debatable are governed by what I call the "pause principle," to which I have referred on certain pages within the text. Generally, the function of the comma is to indicate a slight pause. Therefore, the pause principle suggests that a comma should probably be used if a writer intends a pause between two words when they are spoken aloud. While spoken language does not always follow the same rules that written language follows, and while the pause principle may consequently lead writers in the wrong direction occasionally, the pause principle nonetheless helps *clarify* certain rules throughout the book. I have referred to the pause principle for that purpose.

Throughout the writing process, I have used a number of helpful references. While I take mild issue with a couple of the guidelines found in *The Chicago Manual of Style,* I have deferred to this excellent reference in many cases. I have even supported the positions of *Chicago*'s editors regarding the minor issues about which I have disagreed with them, for *The Chicago Manual of Style* is the best and most authoritative book on English language usage, and I have not been so presumptuous as to think that my work would shift common practice away from *Chicago*'s guidance. I have also periodically referenced a number of the English-language handbooks that I have collected over the years. I am consequently indebted to authors Andrea

## Introduction

Lunsford, Robert Connors, Phillip Gucker, Donald Emery, John Kierzek, Peter Lindblom, Elaine Maimon, Janice Peritz, Kathleen Blake Yancey, Lynn Quitman Troyka, and Douglas Hesse. The clarity of and the examples in some of the books by these writers have often guided me as a professional writer and editor. While I have elaborated on the more general comma instruction provided in their work, I have also been their student.

Finally, I am indebted to a number of students whose patience and careful work have helped me refine and improve various drafts of *The Ultimate Comma Guide*. I am especially grateful to David Amador, Ashley Aulbach, Danielle Bird, Alex Lawhon-Bush, Laine Colarossi, Britnie Jenkins, Hannah Kelley, Lucas Knauss, Greta Larson, Jennifer Goering, Joshua Mathews, Jessica Maxwell, Micah Mitchell, Randi Parrott, Athalee Pate, Lexi Rutberg, Logan Teague, Rebeccah Vetter, Jacqueline Wilkerson, Benjamin Wright, and R.L. Yates.

Whether you are a student in a formal educational setting or an individual who is just trying to improve your writing on your own, I sincerely hope that *The Ultimate Comma Guide* provides answers to your questions about comma usage, that it builds your confidence as a communicator, and that it gives you a greater command of the written sentence.

Gentry Sutton
Oklahoma 2018

# Chapter 1
# Foundational Vocabulary for Comma Instruction

Any instruction about comma usage assumes that the student is equipped with a certain vocabulary, for comma instruction relies on a number of grammatical terms. Many important terms and concepts are defined at relevant places within the chapters of this book. However, many readers may benefit from some "refresher" instruction related to more basic terms and concepts of the English language. This chapter offers such instruction for readers/students who may especially benefit from it. Specifically, this chapter contains a review of parts of speech and the main elements of a sentence.

## 1.A: Parts of Speech

**Nouns**

A **noun** is defined as a person, place, thing, or idea. Nouns may be categorized in a number of ways.

- *Singular or Plural*

The Latin meaning of the word *singular* is, literally, *one*. Consequently, a singular noun is a noun that represents *one* of something. *House, cat, boy, girl, coat, shoe,* and *book* are all singular nouns. The word *plural* simply means *more than one*. The plural form of a noun is usually formed by adding *s* or *es* to the singular form: *houses, cats, boys, girls, shoes, books,* etc. The plural form of a few nouns is formed by changing the actual spelling *within* the noun instead of by adding *s* or *es*. For example, the plural form of *woman* is not *womans*, but *women,* and the plural form of *child* is not

## Chapter 1: Foundational Vocabulary for Comma Instruction

*childs*, but *children*. Such plural formations are called *irregular* plurals because they do not conform to the general *s/es* rule.

- *Count or Noncount*

A count noun is simply a noun that can be counted. *Pennies, dollars, buckets, cars, houses,* and *bicycles* are all count nouns. Noncount nouns cannot be counted. *Air, water, love, butter, grass,* and *dirt* are all noncount nouns. Note that noncount nouns generally do not have plural forms. For example, there cannot be *airs*, only *air*. While we might sometimes use, for example, the word *butters* to compare different brands of butter, what we are really comparing are the brands themselves, not *butters*. That is, if we utter the sentence, "All of the butters in the taste test were made in California," we are actually leaving a word out of the sentence. Grammatically, what we mean is that "All of the butter *brands* (or *varieties*) in the taste test were made in California."

- *Concrete or Abstract*

Concrete nouns can be seen or touched. *Puppy, book, wagon, tire, tree,* and *grass* are concrete nouns. Abstract nouns cannot be seen or touched. *Concept, love, kindness, gentleness, genuineness,* and *belief* are abstract nouns. It might seem at first glance that this category is redundant with the count–noncount category, that abstract and noncount nouns are essentially the same things. Note, however, that some abstract nouns can be counted. People hold any number of *beliefs*, for instance. Additionally, many noncount nouns—*dirt*, for instance—can be touched and are therefore concrete.

- *Common or Proper*

The majority of nouns in the English language are common nouns. They refer to people, places, things, or ideas *in general*. *Athletes, states, buildings,* and *religion* are all common nouns. When these nouns become *specific*, however, they become proper nouns:

Chapter 1: Foundational Vocabulary for Comma Instruction

*Michael Jordan, Oklahoma, Empire State Building,* and *Christianity.* Proper nouns are always capitalized.

- *Collective Nouns*

Collective nouns are nouns that signify a group. *Team, family, class, faculty, group,* and *herd* are all collective nouns. These nouns are singular (one team, one family, one class, etc.), but they signify plurality (more than one person comprises a team, a family, and a class). Collective nouns may be singular or plural, however. For example, consider the following sentence: "The high school basketball *team* on which my nephew plays is as good as some small college basketball *teams.*"

- *Possessive Nouns*

Possessive nouns actually *function* more as adjectives (addressed later in this chapter), though grammarians often classify them as nouns. Possessive nouns contain an apostrophe to show that a certain person, place, thing, or idea "possesses" something else. For example, in the phrase "the cat's toy," *cat's* is a possessive noun. Possessive nouns will be revisited in this chapter's section on adjectives.

**Verbs**

Verbs are words that demonstrate action or a state of being. A sentence cannot be a sentence without at least one verb. There are three main types of verbs: **action** verbs, **helping** verbs, and **linking** verbs.

For most people, **action** verbs are the easiest type of verbs to recognize. The actions that most action verbs signify can be easily pictured in one's mind.

- Jerry *walked* to the park.
- Anita *play*ed the clarinet.
- The girls *ran* to the store.
- The children *watched* a movie.

## Chapter 1: Foundational Vocabulary for Comma Instruction

**Helping** verbs "help" other verbs, while **linking** verbs join a noun or a pronoun (pronouns are addressed later in this chapter) to a word or phrase that renames or describes that noun or pronoun. In other words, linking verbs express a state of being. Table 1.1 below contains a list of helping verbs and linking verbs. Note that some verbs can function as more than one type of verb.

**Table 1.1**
**Helping Verbs and Linking Verbs**

| Helping Verbs | Linking Verbs |
|---|---|
| be, being, been, am, are, is, was, were | be, being, been, am, are, is, was, were |
| do, does, did (may also function as action verbs) | |
| have, had, has (may also function as action verbs) | |
| may, might, must | |
| should, could, would | |
| will, can, shall | |
| | appear, feel, grow, look, make, smell, sound, taste, turn, remain, stay (may also function as action verbs) |
| | become |

The example sentences below may help you understand how certain verbs can function as more than one type of verb.

- My neighbor *was watering* his garden. (The word *was* functions as a helping verb with the action verb *watering*. It "helps" the action verb work.)
- My neighbor *was* an Olympic gymnast. (The word *was* functions as a linking verb. It joins the word *neighbor* to a word that renames it—*gymnast*.)

Chapter 1: Foundational Vocabulary for Comma Instruction

- My neighbor *was* nice to my sister. (The word *was* also functions as a linking verb in this sentence. It joins the word *neighbor* to a word that describes it—*nice*.)
- Nicholas *has played* in the last three games. (The word *has* functions as a helping verb with the action verb *played*. It "helps" the action verb work.)
- Nicholas *has* a cold. (The word *has* functions as an action verb. While it is not an action verb in the same sense that the words *kick* or *throw* are action verbs, it is not a helping verb, nor is it a linking verb (*cold* does not rename or describe *Nicholas*). The best way to categorize *has* in this sentence, then, is as an action verb, for it demonstrates action in the sense that it signifies Nicholas "possessing" something—a cold.)
- The car *sounded* bad. (The word *sounded* functions as a linking verb. It does not express action. Rather, it joins the noun *car* to a word that describes it—*bad*.)
- The trumpeter *sounded* her instrument. (The word *sounded* functions as an action verb in this sentence. It signifies something that the trumpeter *did*.)

**Pronouns**

A **pronoun** is a word that takes the place of a noun or another pronoun. This "other" word is called the pronoun's *antecedent*. Pronouns may be classified as personal, possessive, relative, interrogative, demonstrative, reflexive, intensive, reciprocal, or indefinite.

The *personal* pronouns are *I, me, you, he, she, him, her, it, we, us, they,* and *them*. These pronouns take the place of specific nouns—and sometimes other pronouns.

The *possessive* pronouns are *my, mine, your, yours, her, hers, his, its, our, ours, their,* and *theirs*. These pronouns, like possessive nouns, signify ownership or possession of something.

*Indefinite* pronouns are similar to personal pronouns, but they refer to nonspecific nouns or other pronouns. The indefinite pronouns are *one, everyone, anyone, anybody, anything, everybody, nobody, each, either,*

## Chapter 1: Foundational Vocabulary for Comma Instruction

*neither, no one, none, nothing, somebody, someone, something, both, few, many, several, all, any, more, most,* and *some.*

*Interrogative* pronouns are used with questions. The interrogative pronouns are *who, whoever, whom, whomever, what, whatever, which,* and *whichever.*

The *demonstrative* pronouns are *this, that, these,* and *those.* They often (but not always) point to an antecedent that comes later, whereas most pronouns take the place of a previously stated antecedent. Consider the sentences below.

- Demonstrative pronoun: *This* is a good cake. (The antecedent *book* comes after the pronoun *this.*)
- Personal pronoun: Pedro went home after *he* left the supermarket. (The antecedent *Pedro* comes before the pronoun *he.*)

Sometimes, especially in speech, a demonstrative pronoun may not have an antecedent.

- *These* are too tight.

*Relative* pronouns begin certain dependent clauses, which will be defined in the next chapter. Most of the relative pronouns—*who, whoever, whom, whomever, what, whatever, which, whichever*—can also be interrogative pronouns, but they function differently. *That* is also a common relative pronoun.

- The pencil *that* broke is now in the trash can.

*Reflexive* pronouns end in *–self* or *–selves* and simply refer back to another word so that a sentence can make sense.

- The boys taught *themselves* how to swim.

*Intensive* pronouns also end in *–self* or *–selves.* They are used to create redundancy and add emphasis. They appear infrequently, but writers may find them useful at times.

- The thief *himself* was the one who made the phone call that helped solve the crime.

Finally, the *reciprocal* pronouns *one another* and *each other* are used to refer to compound or plural antecedents.

- My brother and I called *each other* every week when I was in Italy.

In many textbooks about writing, pronouns are afforded a great deal of text—often more than one chapter—because a number of usage issues and common errors are associated with them. Since those issues are not of concern here, they will not be treated in this book. However, being able to distinguish pronouns from other parts of speech is important.

## Adjectives

**Adjectives** describe nouns or pronouns. They bring text to life by specifying color, type, quantity, size, condition, etc. Adjectives are italicized in the sentences below.

- Jackie wore a *blue* dress to the prom. (The word *blue* indicates the color of the dress.)
- The United States values a *democratic* system. (The word *democratic* describes the type of system.)
- Roberto made *four* mistakes on the test. (The word *four* indicates how many mistakes Roberto made.)
- China has a *large* economy. (The word *large* indicates the size of the economy.)
- The *dilapidated* house is about to fall. (The word *dilapidated* describes the condition of the house.)

Usually, adjectives are placed before the nouns or pronouns they modify, as they are in the examples above. However, in sentences with linking verbs, they may also be placed after the words they describe.

## Chapter 1: Foundational Vocabulary for Comma Instruction

- Mr. Billings is *nice*. (The word *nice* describes Mr. Billings.)
- Sharon wore a dress that was *long*. (The word *long* describes the dress.)

Three of the most common words in the English language are actually adjectives. *A, an,* and *the* are special adjectives called *articles*. *The* is called a *definite* article because it points to a specific noun or pronoun; *a* and *an* are *indefinite* articles because they point to nonspecific nouns or pronouns.

- Did you attend *the* reunion?
- I went to *a* play in New York City last summer.
- Julie saw *an* anteater at the zoo.

Sometimes, especially when articles are noted as adjectives, a noun or pronoun may have more than one adjective.

- *The old* piano is in *the living* room. (Both *the* and *old* describe *piano*, and both *the* and *living* describe *room*.)

- *A large* bird is nesting in *an empty oak* tree across the street. (Both *a* and *large* describe *bird*, and *an*, *empty*, and *oak* describe *tree*.)

Even before you arrived at this section in the chapter, you actually studied certain types of words that function as adjectives. Depending on how they are used, possessive nouns, possessive pronouns, demonstrative pronouns, interrogative pronouns, and some indefinite pronouns may be considered adjectives.

- *LaDonna's* car is in the garage. (The word *LaDonna's*, which may also be considered a possessive noun, specifies which car is in the garage.)

Chapter 1: Foundational Vocabulary for Comma Instruction

- *Her* car is in the garage. (The word *her*, which may be a possessive pronoun in some instances, specifies which car is in the garage.)
- *That* car needs to be in a garage. (The word *that*, which may be a demonstrative pronoun in some instances, specifies which car needs to be in a garage.)
- *Which* car needs to be in the garage? (The word *which*, which may be an interrogative pronoun in some instances, points to the word car.)
- *Some* cars on the lawn should be parked in garages. (The word *some*, which may be an indefinite pronoun in some instances, specifies which cars.)

## Adverbs

Like adjectives, **adverb**s are words that describe other words. Whereas adjectives describe nouns and pronouns, however, adverbs describe verbs, adjectives, and other adverbs. Adverbs answer questions such as *when? where? how? to what extent? how much? why? how frequently?* etc. Adverbs most frequently describe verbs. Consider the sentences below.

- The man drove his truck *slowly* across the bridge. (The word *slowly* describes how the man *drove*.)
- The kite sailed *beautifully* in the air. (The word *beautifully* describes how the kite *sailed*.)
- Lisha practiced *diligently* for two years. (The word *diligently* describes how Lisha *practiced*.)
- Jordan *finally* earned an "A" on a test. (The word *finally* describes how/when Jordan *earned*.)
- *Yesterday*, Elizabeth won her first spelling bee. (The word *yesterday* describes when Elizabeth *won*.)
- Jorge played *well* in yesterday's game. (The word *well* describes how Jorge *played*.)

Note from the sentences above that adverbs do not have a fixed place in a sentence when they describe verbs. In other words, they may be placed before or after the verbs they modify.

Also note from the sentences above that adverbs frequently end in *–ly*. Not *all* words that end in *–ly* are adverbs, however, so it is important to consider exactly what word an *–ly* word describes.

- The siblings played a friendly game of catch at the family reunion. (The word *friendly* functions as an adjective in this sentence because it describes *game*, which is a noun.)
- The room was decorated in ghastly colors. (The word *ghastly* functions as an adjective in this sentence because it describes *colors*, which is a noun.)

Adverbs can also describe adjectives. They are usually placed before the adjectives that they describe.

- The Hendersons live in a *nicely* decorated home. (The word *nicely* is an adverb describing *decorated*, which is an adjective describing *home*.)
- Sylvia is driving a *very* new car today. (The word *very* is an adverb describing *new*, which is an adjective describing *car*. In this sentence, the word *today* is also an adverb, for it describes the verb phrase *is driving*.)
- Janice wore a *bright* blue dress to the party last night. (The word *bright* is an adverb describing *blue*, which is an adjective describing *dress*.)

Adverbs can also describe other adverbs.

- He played *very* poorly yesterday. (The word *very* describes *poorly*, which is an adverb describing how he *played*.)
- Tonya sang *really* well in last night's performance. (The word *really* describes *well*, which is an adverb describing how Tonya *sang*.)

- The building was built *quite* hastily because of time demands and budget concerns. (The word *quite* describes *hastily*, which is an adverb describing how the building *was built*.)

Occasionally, adverbs modify the sentiment of an entire thought instead of a specific word. These adverbs usually (but not always) appear at the beginning of a sentence.

- *Unfortunately*, the rainy day prevented the family from enjoying its trip to the zoo.
- *Apparently*, college costs a lot more money than I realized.
- *Interestingly*, Jess prefers playing the drums but is a better guitar player.
- The rainy day prevented the family from enjoying its trip to the zoon, *unfortunately*.

Some adverbs are called **conjunctive adverbs**. Also called **transitional expressions**, these adverbs connect two thoughts and *technically* describe the second (though this definition stretches the meaning of *describe*). As their name implies, conjunctive adverbs are closely associated with conjunctions (addressed later in this chapter), but they will be classified as adverbs in this book. Table 1.2 contains the most common conjunctive adverbs.

**Table 1.2**
**Common Conjunctive Adverbs**

| again | next | likewise |
|---|---|---|
| also | nevertheless | consequently |
| first | however | similarly |
| hence | thus | therefore |
| second | indeed | instead |
| furthermore | third | of course |
| meanwhile | moreover | nonetheless |

Finally, be aware that *not, no, only, almost, too,* and *never* are adverbs. (The word *no* may also be classified as an interjection, depending on how it is used. Interjections are addressed later in this chapter.)

**Prepositions**

A **preposition** connects a noun or a pronoun to another word in a sentence, usually to demonstrate a relationship in time or space. A preposition begins a *prepositional phrase*, which is a pair or a group of words that, together, function as an adjective or an adverb. (Prepositional phrases may function as nouns, but only rarely.) While a prepositional phrase begins with a preposition, it ends with a noun or a pronoun, which is called the *object* of the prepositional phrase. Many prepositional phrases contain adjectives that describe the object. As Table 1.3 demonstrates, most prepositions are short words. Some prepositions, however, are compound, consisting of two words.

**Table 1.3**
**Common Prepositions**

| according to | because of | out of |
|---|---|---|
| along | across | alongside |
| alongside of | instead of | together with |
| behind | between | by |
| below | inside | in |
| beneath | of | for |
| due to | such as | like |
| into | against | beside |
| off | beyond | among |
| onto | during | at |
| over | under | around |
| through | up | on |
| up to | as of | aside from |
| with | without | until |

The following sentences contain prepositional phrases and some explanation about them.

Chapter 1: Foundational Vocabulary for Comma Instruction

- Jerry played his guitar **for three hours**.

    (The preposition *for* begins the prepositional phrase. The word *hours* is the object of the preposition. The word *three* functions as an adjective that describes *hours*. The entire prepositional phrase functions as an adverb because it describes the verb *played*; that is, it communicates *how long* Jerry played.)

- Andrea found the treasure **under the oak tree** that is **in the back yard**.

    (The word *under* is the preposition in the first prepositional phrase. The word *tree* is the object of the phrase. The words *the* and *oak* function as adjectives that describe *tree*. The entire phrase functions as an adverb because it describes the verb *found*; that is, it communicates *where* Andrea found the treasure.

    The word *in* is the preposition in the second prepositional phrase. The word *yard* is the object of the phrase. The words *the* and *back* function as adjectives that describe *yard*. The entire phrase functions as an adjective because it describes the noun *tree*.)

- The softball game **in Springfield** was cancelled **due to the close lightning**.

    (The word *in* begins the first prepositional phrase. The word *Springfield* is the object of the phrase. Note that this particular prepositional phrase does not contain any words that describe the object. The entire phrase functions as an adjective because it describes the noun *game*.

    The compound preposition *due to* begins the second prepositional phrase. The word *lightning* is the object of the phrase. The words *the* and *close* function as adjectives that describe *lightning*. The entire phrase functions as an adverb because it describes the verb phrase *was cancelled*; that is, it communicates *why* the game was cancelled.)

## Conjunctions

**Conjunctions** connect words or groups of words. The three main types of conjunctions are *coordinating* conjunctions, *correlative* conjunctions, and *subordinating* conjunctions. Subordinating conjunctions are used with *dependent clauses*, which are not defined until the next chapter. Consequently, subordinating conjunctions will be addressed in chapter 2 rather than here. Understanding coordinating and correlative conjunctions, however, will help you understand the essence of the conjunction's function.

Just as you might *coordinate* your shirt or blouse with the rest of your outfit, coordinating conjunctions are used to connect two or more elements that have the same grammatical form: nouns with nouns, adjectives with adjectives, adverbs with adverbs, complete thoughts with complete thoughts, etc. Only seven coordinating conjunctions exist in the English language. They can easily be memorized with the use of the mnemonic device FANBOYS, which stands for *For, And, Nor, But, Or, Yet,* and *So*. In the examples below, note how the coordinating conjunctions are used to link elements of the same grammatical form.

- Jimmy *and* Lisa went on a date last night. (The coordinating conjunction *and* connects two proper nouns.)
- Dana could not remember if the car was black *or* blue. (The coordinating conjunction *or* connects two adjectives.)
- The drummer of the band performed poorly *yet* passionately. (The coordinating conjunction *yet* connects two adverbs.)
- Harper did not write a good essay, *but* he did score well on the multiple-choice part of the exam. (The coordinating conjunction *but* connects two complete thoughts.)

*Correlative* conjunctions are basically coordinating conjunctions that come in pairs: *either…or, neither…nor, both…and, not only…but also*. The sentences below contain correlative conjunctions.

- Raymond played *both* the trumpet *and* the piano in last night's concert. (The correlative conjunction *both…and* connects two nouns.)

## Chapter 1: Foundational Vocabulary for Comma Instruction

- The cat was *not only* exhausted *but also* sick. (The correlative conjunction *not only…but also* connects two adjectives.)
- Unfortunately, the guest speaker spoke *neither* eloquently *nor* clearly. (The correlative conjunction *neither…nor* connects two adverbs.)
- Nicholas was *either* nervous about being the center of attention, *or* he simply failed to prepare himself adequately for the challenge. (The correlative conjunction *either…or* connects two thoughts.)

**Interjections**

The last part of speech is the **interjection**. Often, interjections communicate surprise or strong emotion and are written alone with an exclamation point.

- *Wow*! Did you see that fish?
- *Yikes*! I almost fell out of the boat!

An interjection is not always followed by an exclamation point, though, and everyday words such as *yes* and *no* are categorized as interjections as well.

- *Yes*, you may have a cookie.
- *No*, you may not have a cookie.

Table 1.4 contains a number of common interjections. You probably know of other interjections that are regional or colloquial.

Chapter 1: Foundational Vocabulary for Comma Instruction

**Table 1.4**
**Common Interjections**

| Absolutely | Aha | Alas |
|---|---|---|
| All right | Bravo | My goodness |
| Gee | Oh My | Hey |
| Gosh | Ha | Oops |
| Hmm | No | Ugh |
| Oh | Ooh | Yes |
| Ouch | Shucks | Whew |
| Uh-oh | Whee | Yay |
| Whoa | Wow | Boo |
| Yikes | Ah | Yuck |

# 1.B: Subjects and Predicates

All complete sentences contain a **subject** and a **predicate**. The subject is the person or thing the sentence is about, and it may include descriptive words about that person or thing. The predicate is the group of words that communicates something about the subject, explaining what the subject is, was, is doing, was doing, etc. The *simple subject* is the single word that is the heart of the subject. *The simple subject must be a noun or a pronoun, and it cannot be in a prepositional phrase.* In the example sentence above, the simple subject is *store*. The *simple predicate* is the main verb or verb phrase that communicates the action or the state of being of the subject. In the most common types of sentences, the subject begins the sentence and the predicate follows. Where appropriate in this book, subjects will be underlined once and predicates will be underlined twice.

- A silver horse pranced across the arena.

In the sentence above, *A silver horse* is the complete subject of the sentence, and *horse* is the simple subject. *A silver horse* is what the sentence is about. The words *pranced across the arena* comprise the complete predicate, and *pranced* is the simple predicate. These words explain what the horse did.

Chapter 1: Foundational Vocabulary for Comma Instruction

A slightly longer sentence is below.

- The grocery store in the neighboring town is having a great sale on peaches today.

In this sentence, *The grocery store in the neighboring town* is the *thing* that the sentence is about, so this group of words constitutes the complete subject. The simple subject is *store*. The word group *is having a great sale on peaches today* constitutes the complete predicate because it communicates what the subject is doing. The simple predicate is *is having*.

Consider another example:

- The family's vacation to the Rocky Mountains was postponed because of a severe snow storm.

In the sentence above, the complete subject is *The family's vacation to the Rocky Mountains*, and the simple subject is *vacation* (a noun/thing). The complete predicate is *was postponed because of a severe snow storm*, and the simple predicate is the phrase *was postponed* (a verb phrase in which *was* is a helping verb for the main action verb *postponed*).

Sometimes a sentence may contain a compound subject, a compound predicate, or both.

- Jack and Jill went up the hill. (*Jack* and *Jill* constitute a compound subject.)
- Brady washed and vacuumed his new car last week. (The words *washed* and *vacuumed* constitute a compound predicate.)
- Samantha and Sherry sang and danced in the fall production of *The Music Man*. (*Samantha* and *Sherry* constitute a compound subject, and *sang* and *danced* constitute a compound predicate.)

Sometimes a sentence may have multiple subjects and predicates because it contains two distinct thoughts.

- Samantha performed a tap dance in the spring musical, and Sherry played in the orchestra pit.

## Chapter 1: Foundational Vocabulary for Comma Instruction

Of course, not all sentences in the English language follow the pattern of the sentences above. That is, not all sentences begin with a subject and end with a predicate. Sometimes the predicate may be transposed or split.

- <u>Into the ocean went</u> <u>the anxious diver</u>. (The predicate is transposed; it comes first.)
- <u>After the movie,</u> <u>Fernando</u> <u>told his date about his crazy day</u>. (The predicate is split. The prepositional phrase *after the movie* logically goes with the predicate, not the subject, for it explains when Fernando *told*.)

In the case of a sentence that expresses a command, the subject is said to be what grammarians call the "understood *you.*" For example, in the sentence *Clean your room before dinner,* a subject is not explicitly stated. However, it is *understood* that the individual who is spoken/written to is the one who is supposed to clean his or her room. When identifying the subject for an exercise, the "understood *you*" is placed in parentheses.

- <u>(You)</u> <u>Clean your room before dinner</u>.

To find the subject of a sentence that begins with the word *there*, you may find it helpful to ask who or what the verb is referring to and then rearrange the sentence to eliminate or move the word *there*. Consider the examples below.

- There is snow on the ground at my grandfather's house. (What *is* on the ground? *Snow.* <u>Snow</u> <u>is on the ground [there] at my grandfather's house</u>.)
- There went Raymond on his skateboard. (Who *went*? *Raymond.* <u>Raymond</u> <u>went [there] on his skateboard</u>.)

Chapter 1: Foundational Vocabulary for Comma Instruction

# 1.C: Predicate Complements

You have probably noticed that a sentence does not usually end immediately after the verb, or simple predicate. Most of the time, verbs have **predicate complements** that comprise part of the predicate and come after the verb. Predicate complements are classified and named according to their function and what type of verb they follow.

Recall from this chapter's section on verbs that a linking verb is a verb that links a noun or a pronoun (more specifically, the simple subject) to a word that describes or renames it. The word that describes or renames the subject is a predicate complement. If the complement describes the subject, it is a called a *predicate adjective*. If the complement renames the subject, it is called a *predicate nominative*.

- The shirt on the floor <u>is *clean*</u>. (The word *clean* is a predicate adjective because it describes *shirt*.)
- Jessie's achievement <u>was a huge *boost* to her confidence</u>. (The word *boost* is a predicate nominative because it is a noun that renames *achievement*.)

Whereas linking verbs usually have predicate adjectives or predicate nominatives, action verbs often have *direct* or *indirect objects*. Objects follow *transitive* action verbs, which are verbs that require a person or thing upon which the verb acts. For example, *Jenny picked* does not make sense (unless it is in an unusual context, such as being the response to the question, Who picked?). The verb *picked* needs an object. In the sentence *Jenny picked blueberries at her grandparents' house,* the word *blueberries* is the object. More specifically, *blueberries* is a *direct object*; it is the receiver of the action *picked*. For clarity, a few more sentences containing direct objects are below. The direct objects are in boldface type.

- <u>Johnny moved</u> the **furniture** from the living room to the bedroom.
- <u>Kristen earned</u> good **grades** last semester.
- <u>Richard mowed</u> the **lawn** and then <u>watered</u> the **garden**.

## Chapter 1: Foundational Vocabulary for Comma Instruction

Sometimes transitive verbs take both direct objects and *indirect objects*. An indirect object is the word that represents *to whom* or *for whom* (or *to what* or *for what*) the action was done. Indirect objects are common with verbs such as *ask, tell, write, send, make, sell, sing, give* and their various forms.

- Larry wrote *Lori* a long *letter*. (The word *letter* is the direct object because it is the receiver of the action *wrote*. The word *Lori* is the indirect object because it communicates the person for whom the letter was written.)
- My uncle Roger told the *audience* an engaging *story* about courage and compassion. (The word *story* is the direct object because it is the receiver of the action *told*. The word *audience* is the indirect object because it communicates the people for whom the story was told.)
- Carefully, the fireman handed the little *girl* the rescued *kitten*. (The word *kitten* is the direct object because it is the receiver of the action *handed*. The word *girl* is the indirect object because it communicates the person to whom the kitten was handed.)
- The evil queen asked the crystal *ball* a *question* about the future. (The word *question* is the direct object because it is the receiver action *asked*. The word *ball* is the indirect object because it communicates the thing to which the question was directed.)

Remember that not all transitive verbs require both an indirect object and a direct object. They do, however, all require at least a direct object, and some sentences may have compound objects.

- On his way home, Brandon ignored two red *lights* and one stop *sign*. (The words *lights* and *sign* are both direct objects because they are the receivers of the action *ignored*. The sentence does not need an indirect object.)

As stated at the beginning of this chapter, comma instruction by necessity makes use of some fundamental grammatical terms. Understanding the basic concepts and terminology presented in this chapter will benefit you as you encounter this book's instruction about

Chapter 1: Foundational Vocabulary for Comma Instruction

various comma rules—particularly in chapter 9, but also in other chapters.

# Chapter 2
# Independent and Dependent Clauses

If you can understand the difference between **independent** and **dependent** clauses, you can use commas correctly the majority of the time. To understand the difference between these two types of clauses, however, you must first understand what is meant by the word **clause**. To gain this understanding, it is helpful to contrast clauses with **phrases**.

## 2.A: Clauses vs. Phrases

A clause is a group of words that contains both a subject and a verb. Clauses may or may not be complete sentences.

-     S   V
- before he went to the store
-  S  V
- Lucy has a nice wardrobe.
-      S   V
- As the crow flies
-  S  V
- Frogs croak more at night.
-     S    V
- that Henry was wearing

All of the word groups above are **clauses** because they contain both a subject and a verb. Three of the examples above are not complete sentences, but they could contribute to complete sentences if they were used appropriately:

Chapter 2: Independent and Dependent Clauses

- John fed his dog *before he went to the store.*
- *As the crow flies,* Oklahoma City is approximately one hundred miles from Tulsa.
- Jill spilled a soft drink on the shirt *that Henry was wearing.*

A clause is different from a **phrase** in that a phrase is a group of words that does *not* contain both a subject and a verb. A few examples of phrases are included in Table 2.1.

**Table 2.1**
**Examples of Phrases**

| Phrase | Phrase Used in a Sentence |
|---|---|
| on the phone | Jared typed his paper while he talked *on the phone.* |
| barn wood | Shelly bought some used *barn wood* at the yard sale. |
| expensive concert tickets | The band's *expensive concert tickets* were worth the price. |
| annoyed with his little sister | *Annoyed with his little sister,* Jeremy left the room. |
| to go | The team wanted *to go* to the championship. |
| was walking | Cassandra *was walking* when her cell phone rang. |

Many different types of phrases exist, and you would do well to learn about them. In fact, you will learn about most of them in chapter 3. For now, however, you will benefit greatly from simply understanding the difference between a phrase and a clause.

## 2.B: Independent and Dependent Clauses

Now that you understand the definition of a clause, you can understand the difference between an **independent** and a **dependent** clause. When it comes to mastering comma usage—and writing good

## Chapter 2: Independent and Dependent Clauses

sentences—the ability to recognize independent and dependent clauses is one of the most important abilities you can have.

An **independent clause** is a clause that can stand alone. In other words, it *could* function as a complete sentence, even if it does not. Independent clauses are italicized in the sentences below.

- Before he started grilling, *Joe prepared each steak with his favorite seasonings.*
- Because the rain soaked the field, *the game has been postponed until tomorrow.*

In the examples above, the italicized word groups are independent clauses because they could function as complete sentences on their own.

- Joe prepared each steak with his favorite seasonings.
- The game has been postponed until tomorrow.

A **dependent clause,** also called a **subordinate clause,** *cannot* function alone as a complete sentence. Like a child is *subordinate* to his or her parents, a dependent clause is subordinate to an independent clause somewhere in the sentence. In other words, it needs an independent clause in order to function properly. Consider again the examples used above:

- *Before he started grilling,* Joe prepared each steak with his favorite seasonings.
- *Because the rain the soaked the field,* the game has been postponed until tomorrow.

The italicized word groups in the examples above are dependent clauses. While the italicized group of words in the first sentence contains a subject (he) and a verb (started grilling), the thought is incomplete. What happened before he started grilling? Did he take a nap? Did he call his wife? We don't know unless we read the independent clause that follows. In the second sentence, *Because the rain soaked the field* contains a subject (rain) and verb (soaked), but this clause is also incomplete. What happened because the rain soaked the field? The independent clause that follows the dependent clause is needed in order to make the sentence complete.

As in the examples above, dependent clauses are often found at the beginning of sentences. They may be found anywhere in a sentence, however. Consider:

- People should obtain permits *if they wish to park in reserved spots.*
- The course was taught by the man *who wore flannel ties every day.*

The italicized word groups in the two sentences above contain both a subject (*they; who*) and a verb (*wish; wore*), but they could not stand alone.

Dependent clauses can be noun clauses, adverb clauses, or adjective clauses. Being able to identify a clause's function is not too important, but being able to recognize the individual words that often begin each type of clause will help you a great deal. Dependent clauses that are adverb clauses modify verbs, adjectives, or other adverbs and often begin with **subordinating conjunctions.** Recall from chapter 1 that subordinating conjunctions were mentioned but not addressed in depth. Like coordinating conjunction and correlative conjunctions (see chapter 1), subordinating conjunctions join sentence elements, but unlike other conjunctions, they do *not* join elements of the same grammatical form. In fact, subordinating conjunctions are so named because they *subordinate* one thought to another. In other words, they introduce a dependent (or subordinate clause), which cannot stand without an independent clause. Some of the most common subordinating conjunctions are in Table 2.2. Being able to recognize them can help you distinguish dependent clauses from independent clauses.

Chapter 2: Independent and Dependent Clauses

**Table 2.2**
**Common Subordinating Conjunctions**

| after | although | as | as if |
|---|---|---|---|
| as long as | as much as | as soon as | as though |
| because | before | even though | if |
| even if | how | now that | lest |
| in order that | once | since | so that |
| provided (that) | though | whenever | wherever |
| than | that | unless | while |
| until | when | where | however |
| whereas | in case | as soon as | whether |

The sentence below contains a dependent clause that begins with a subordinating conjunction. The entire dependent clause is italicized.

- People should obtain permits *if they wish to park in reserved spots*.

The word *if* in the sentence above is a subordinating conjunction that introduces a dependent clause functioning as an adverb. The clause is an adverb clause because it expresses a condition of the verb phrase *should obtain*.

Consider another example:

- His cereal was crunchier *than it was yesterday morning*.

In this sentence, *than* is a subordinating conjunction that introduces a dependent clause functioning as an adverb. The clause is an adverb clause because it modifies an adjective—*crunchier*.

Adverbial dependent clauses address questions of time, place, cause, purpose, manner, condition, result, concession, or comparison from a main/independent clause.

- TIME: I played baseball *when I was a child*. (The subordinating conjunction *when* introduces a dependent clause that describes *when* the subject *played*.)

- PLACE: *Wherever he goes*, he will remember her. (The subordinating conjunction *wherever* introduces a dependent clause that describes *where* the subject will *remember*.)
- CAUSE: *Since Alex earned good grades this semester*, his parents are rewarding him. (The subordinating conjunction *since* introduces a dependent clause that describes the *reason* that Alex's parents are *rewarding* him.)
- PURPOSE: Betty worked hard *so that she could keep her job*. (The subordinating conjunction *so that* introduces a dependent clause that explains *why* she *worked* hard.)
- MANNER: Rachel entered the room *as if she were surprised*. (The subordinating conjunction *as if* introduces a dependent clause that explains *how* Rachel *entered* the room.)
- CONDITION: The game will not continue *unless the storm passes*. (The subordinating conjunction *unless* introduces a dependent clause that places a *condition* on whether the game will *continue*.)
- RESULT: Richard was so tired *that he fell asleep immediately*. (The subordinating conjunction *that* introduces a dependent clause that explains the *result* of Jared being so *tired*. Note that this particular adverbial dependent clause describes the adjective *tired*, whereas the other dependent clauses in the examples above describe verbs.)
- CONCESSION: *Even though I like the car*, I will not buy it. (The subordinating conjunction *even though* introduces a dependent clause that concedes a point to the main clause.)
- COMPARISON: Brooke's paper was better *than Candy's was*. (The subordinating conjunction *than* introduces a dependent clause that compares Candy's paper to the adjective describing Brooke's paper—*better*.)

Dependent clauses that are adjective clauses modify nouns and usually begin with **relative pronouns**—*who, whom, whose, which, that,* etc. (table 2.3). Occasionally, adjective clauses begin with *when, where,* or *why*.

## Chapter 2: Independent and Dependent Clauses

**Table 2.3**
**Relative Pronouns**

| who | whoever | whom | whomever |
|---|---|---|---|
| whose | what | whatever | which |
| whichever | that | | |

- The purple car, *which was parked illegally,* had a ticket on its windshield.
- Lloyd, *who has a great voice,* sings bass in a local quartet.
- The monkey *that is in the tree* is throwing bananas.

If the dependent clauses in the above sentences were not italicized, you could still recognize them by understanding that every verb must have a subject. In the last sentence, *is throwing* is the main verb/verb phrase, and its obvious subject is *monkey*. Recognizing the other *is* should tell you that another clause exists in the sentence. That is, every verb has to have a subject. But what is the dependent clause's subject? Since a pronoun takes the place of a noun and can therefore be the subject of a sentence or a clause, the relative pronoun *that* functions as the subject of the clause. Similarly, in the other two sentences above, *which* and *who* function as the subjects of the dependent clauses. The clauses are dependent, of course, because they cannot stand alone as complete sentences. The italicized clauses are *adjective clauses* because they modify the words *car, Lloyd,* and *monkey,* respectively, all of which are nouns. Notice from the three sentences above that an adjective clause often "splits" an independent clause. *The purple car had a ticket on its windshield* is an independent clause, but the clause is interrupted by the adjective clause *which was parked illegally*. Similarly, *Lloyd sings bass in a local quartet* is an independent clause that is interrupted by the adjective clause *who has a great voice*.

Many times, the relative pronoun does not function as a clause's subject: it merely introduces the dependent clause.

- The dress *that Jessica wore to the ball* was beautiful.

## Chapter 2: Independent and Dependent Clauses

In the dependent clause above, the subject is *Jessica*, but the relative pronoun *that* signals the beginning of a dependent clause.

A dependent clause that is a noun clause also usually begins with a relative pronoun. In chapter 1 you studied subjects and objects as one-word entities. Sometimes, however, an entire noun clause—not just a single word—may function as a subject or as an object.

- *That he was the best boxer in the world* was common knowledge. (The entire noun clause functions as the subject of the sentence.)
- *Why he went to the police* is a mystery. (The entire noun clause functions as the subject of the sentence.)
- Mrs. Wilson told us *that she was quitting*. (The entire noun clause functions as a direct object.)
- I will buy dinner for *whoever wins the game*. (The entire noun clause functions as the object of the preposition *for*.)

In these examples, the italicized clauses could not stand alone. The italicized word groups are therefore dependent clauses, and since they occupy places that nouns usually occupy, they are **noun clauses** that are introduced by the relative pronouns *that, why, that,* and *whoever,* respectively. We will not concern ourselves any further with noun clauses, but you will benefit from being able to recognize them.

Now that you can distinguish an independent clause from a dependent clause, you are ready to learn the first rule of comma usage.

> Comma Rule #1: A sentence comprised of two independent clauses or complete thoughts should be joined by both a comma and a coordinating conjunction, and the comma should be placed immediately after the first clause or complete thought.

Independent clauses can be joined with a semicolon or a period (they are, of course, treated as two complete sentences when they are joined with a period), but they are often connected by a **coordinating conjunction** and a comma. Table 2.4 contains the seven coordinating

## Chapter 2: Independent and Dependent Clauses

conjunctions of the English language. Recall from Chapter 1 that using the mnemonic device FANBOYS can help you memorize the coordinating conjunctions.

**Table 2.4**
**The Seven Coordinating Conjunctions**

| For | And | Nor | But | Or | Yet | So |
|---|---|---|---|---|---|---|

In the sentence below, the word *but* is the coordinating conjunction.

- Shannon likes basketball the best, *but* she is a better softball player.

Note that a comma is placed *before* a coordinating conjunction—not after. Also note that Comma Rule #1 refers to "two independent clauses" or "complete thoughts." As mentioned above, not all dependent clauses are adverb clauses. Some dependent clauses are adjective clauses, and sometimes dependent clauses "finish" independent clauses to make them complete thoughts. Consider the two sentences below.

- The monkey *that is in the tree* is throwing bananas, and zoo-goers *who are watching* are laughing.
- The dress *that Jessica wore to the ball* was beautiful, and the necklace *that her father gave her* matched it perfectly.

The italicized word groups are clauses because they have both a subject and a verb, but they could not stand alone as complete thoughts, so they are dependent clauses. However, they "complete" the independent clauses in the sentences and are thus "part" of complete thoughts. In these sentences, the commas and coordinating conjunctions join complete thoughts, not *just* independent clauses.

## Chapter 2: Independent and Dependent Clauses

When independent clauses or complete thoughts are joined with *only a comma,* an error called a **comma splice** occurs.

- *Incorrect*: He went to the store, she went to the game.
- *Correct*: He went to the store, *but* she went to the game.

Chapter 9 deals with the problem of the comma splice in more detail.

When independent clauses are joined with neither a comma nor a coordinating conjunction, an error called a **run-on sentence** occurs. This error is so named because it signifies that two complete sentences have "run on" together with no punctuation.

- *Incorrect*: He went to the store she went to the game.
- *Correct*: He went to the store, *but* she went to the game.

Each sentence below contains two independent clauses or complete thoughts that are properly connected with coordinating conjunctions and commas.

- Jerry watched television all night, and Robert went to bed early.
- The Braves won the game, but the Red Sox made fewer errors.
- Natalie did not pass her driving test, nor did Shelly pass her written test.
- Teachers should be paid more money, for they are invaluable to society.
- Greg will ride the bike that he received as a birthday gift, or his sister will take him to school.
- The exterminator set six of the best traps that are available on the market, yet the mouse continues to be a pest.
- The bank in his hometown would not accept his check, so Lou was forced to drive ten miles to the nearest ATM machine.

Some sentences contain three or more independent clauses or complete thoughts. When the clauses are equal in authority and function as serial items (see chapter 5), they should simply be

## Chapter 2: Independent and Dependent Clauses

punctuated as other serial items are punctuated. As noted in chapter 5, a *series* is a group of *three or more* words, phrases, or clauses that appear within a sentence and have the same grammatical form. Serial items should be separated by commas, and the word *and* (or occasionally the word *or*) should appear between the last two items.

- The boys ran through fields, yards, and parking lots. (series of objects of the preposition *through*)
- The Bears won on Sunday, the Cubs won on Monday, and the Bulls won on Tuesday. (series of independent clauses that are equal in authority)

Sometimes the independent clauses or complete thoughts in a sentence with three or more are *not* equal in authority. We cannot punctuate them as serial items because they are not serial items. Likewise, separating each independent clause or complete thought with both a coordinating conjunction and a comma (as in Comma Rule #1) may unnecessarily interrupt the flow of a sentence with three or more independent clauses or complete thoughts that are not equal, especially if the clauses or complete thoughts are relatively short. Consider the sentence below:

- The party has ended, and everyone has left, so Melissa must now clean up the house.

Even though *The party has ended* and *everyone has left* are independent clauses, the comma between them suggests a short pause that would probably not be observed if the sentence were spoken. The pause would probably not be observed because the three independent clauses are not equal in authority. In essence, the first two clauses function *together* to state the *reason* for the action expressed in the third clause, *Melissa must now clean up the house*. Consequently, the sentence would be punctuated more accurately if the first comma were removed.

- The party has ended and everyone has left, so Melissa must now clean up the house.

## Chapter 2: Independent and Dependent Clauses

Occasionally, a sentence may have four independent clauses or complete thoughts, two of which function together in relationship to the other two.

- *Composition II is a lot of work* and *Introduction to Physics is very difficult*, so *I am dropping out of school* and *I am going to start my own business.*
- *Shopping exhausts me* and *mowing makes me hungry*, but *watching movies relaxes me* and *coffee suppresses my appetite.*

Sentences such as the ones above are rare. If you must write them, however, observe Comma Rule #2.

---

Comma Rule #2: When a sentence contains three or more independent clauses or complete thoughts and two of them function as compound elements that express cause, effect, or contrast in relationship to the other(s), the comma between the like clauses or complete thoughts should usually be omitted, especially if the clauses or complete thoughts are short.

---

- *Mr. Santana allowed students to catch up on late work* and *Mrs. Lopez showed a film clip*, so *Alex did not have a very demanding day at school.* (The first two clauses function together to express cause.)
- *A lot of rain fell all night*, so *the game was cancelled* and *the other team went home.* (The last two clauses express effect.)
- *Jeremy studied hard* and *Amy went to class all semester*, yet *they both failed.* (The first two clauses contrast with the third.)
- *Sandy gardened all day* and *Grandpa fixed the car*, but *Grandma did nothing.* (The first two clauses contrast with the third.)
- *The walls are black* and *the carpet is pink*, but *the curtains are red* and *the trim is green.* (The first two clauses contrast "equally" with the last two clauses.)

Like Comma Rule #2, the next rule also revolves around an exception to using a comma between two independent clauses or

## Chapter 2: Independent and Dependent Clauses

complete thoughts that are joined by a coordinating conjunction. In the next chapter, you will learn about how commas are placed after introductory elements—prepositional phrases, dependent clauses, and other special words and word groups that begin sentences. For now, observe Comma Rule #3.

---

Comma Rule #3: When a pair of independent clauses or complete thoughts follows an introductory element that requires a comma, and when the introductory element modifies both clauses, the comma between the two independent clauses should usually be omitted.

---

- Since you don't know the city very well, you should not talk to strangers and you should not enter any strange buildings. (The dependent clause *Since you don't know the city very well* expresses the reason for the instruction in both of the independent clauses that follow.)
- With much anxiety, Sam returned to his seat and Jill awaited the verdict. (If the prepositional phrase *With much anxiety* is intended to modify both of the independent clauses that follow, then the comma between the independent clauses should be omitted. However, if the prepositional phrase is meant to modify only the first independent clause—*Sam returned to his seat*—then a comma should be used to separate the independent clauses, as in the sentence below.)

    o   With much anxiety, Sam returned to his seat, and Jill awaited the verdict.

- Carefully, Bailey crept into the yard and her partner secured the entryway. (If the adverb *Carefully* is intended to modify both of the independent clauses that follow, then the comma between the independent clauses should be omitted. However, if *Carefully* is meant to modify only the first independent clause—*Bailey crept into the yard*—then a comma should be used to separate the independent clauses, as in the example below.)

## Chapter 2: Independent and Dependent Clauses

> o Carefully, Bailey crept into the yard, and her partner secured the entryway.

So far, you have learned about comma issues related to independent clauses. Now it is time to learn about comma usage as it relates to dependent clauses.

---
Comma Rule #4: *Generally*, a comma should follow a sentence-beginning dependent clause that begins with a subordinating conjunction and is followed by an independent clause.

---

Understanding Comma Rule #4 is all about understanding that the location of a dependent clause often determines whether or not a comma should be used with it. Consider the sentences below.

- Doug drove to campus to register for classes *after he finished cleaning the interior of his car*.
- *After he finished cleaning the interior of his car*, Doug drove to campus to register for classes.

Although both of the sentences above communicate the same information, only one of the sentences contains a comma. In both of the sentences above, the clause *Doug drove to campus to register for classes* is an independent clause because it can stand alone as a complete sentence. However, the clause *after he finished cleaning the interior of his car* is a dependent clause. It contains a subject (he) and a verb (finished cleaning), but it cannot stand alone as a sentence. The subordinating conjunction *after* implies that the sentence has more to communicate. In other words, we wonder *what happened* after Doug finished cleaning his car. Because of Comma Rule #4, a comma is used only in the second sentence, the sentence in which the dependent clause comes first.

Possible exceptions to this rule apply to sentences that begin with *short* dependent clauses and to sentences in which the independent clause that follows the dependent clause is significantly shorter than the dependent clause itself. Even in these cases, however, you will not be wrong to use a comma.

## Chapter 2: Independent and Dependent Clauses

- *Before he left*, he mowed the lawn and repaired his son's wagon.
  or
- *Before he left* he mowed the lawn and repaired his son's wagon. (The introductory dependent clause is short.)


- *Since Greg offered a sincere apology*, Mike forgave him.
  or
- *Since Greg offered a sincere apology* Mike forgave him. (The independent clause that follows the introductory dependent clause is shorter.)

Just for clarity, consider a few more sentences that are governed by Comma Rule #4.

- *While he cleaned his room*, he found homework assignments from his seventh-grade year.
- *Since Austin is a long way from Kansas City*, the couple decided to book a flight.
- *Before she told her mother about the accident*, Sherry carefully considered the advantages and disadvantages of being completely truthful.

Note that Comma Rule #4 specifies dependent clauses that begin with subordinating conjunctions. A dependent clause that functions as a noun and therefore begins with a relative pronoun does not necessarily need a comma if it begins a sentence.

- *Whatever information you can offer* <u>would be</u> useful. (The dependent clause begins with the relative pronoun *whatever*—not a subordinating conjunction—and therefore functions as the subject of the sentence—that is, a noun clause.)

As stated in the information about Comma Rule #4, when a dependent clause *follows* an independent clause, a comma is not usually needed to separate the two clauses.

## Chapter 2: Independent and Dependent Clauses

- He found homework assignments from his seventh-grade year *while he cleaned his room.*
- Sherry carefully considered the advantages and disadvantages of being completely truthful *before she told her mother about the accident.*
- The couple decided to book a flight *since Austin is a long way from Kansas City.*

There are occasions, however, when it *is* appropriate to place a comma after an independent clause that is followed by a dependent clause. The most common of these occasions revolve around comma rules pertaining to *nonrestrictive elements*, which are addressed in Chapter 4. Nonetheless, two specific occasions are cited in Comma Rules #5 and #6.

---

Comma Rule #5: *Generally*, a comma is not necessary after a sentence-beginning independent clause or complete thought that is followed by a dependent clause. However, when an adverbial dependent clause follows an independent clause or complete thought and the dependent clause communicates a contrast, exception, condition, or other sentiment that the writer wishes to emphasize with a pause, a comma may separate the clauses.

---

- Don't go to the party, since you might get in trouble if you do.
- Jackie played the cello, whereas Ben played the tuba.
- You may come in the house, though you might want to clean your shoes before you do.
- All students should submit the assignment, even if they are not finished with it.

## Chapter 2: Independent and Dependent Clauses

> Comma Rule #6: *Generally,* a comma is not necessary after a sentence-beginning independent clause or complete thought that is followed by a dependent clause. However, a comma may be used after an independent clause or complete thought that is followed by a dependent clause when the sentence and the clauses within it are long and a comma would therefore facilitate a natural pause if the sentence were read aloud.

Consider the sentence below, in which the last dependent clause is italicized.

- If a college wants to offer a degree in history with emphasis in teaching licensure, it will need to answer a number of important questions, and it will need to seek formal approval from its accrediting agency and from all internal governing officials, *since a history degree with emphasis in teaching licensure is an entirely different degree.*

In the sentence above, a comma is placed before the italicized dependent clause even though it is preceded by an independent clause. Note, however, the word *may* in Comma Rule #6. In other words, the final comma is optional. In choosing whether to use a comma in such a situation, a writer should consider whether a short pause would be included if the sentence were spoken. In such a long a sentence, the meeting point of the final two clauses might serve as a natural place for the speaker to take a short breath.

The final comma rule of this chapter is needed for sentences that begin with consecutive dependent clauses.

> Comma Rule #7: When a pair of dependent clauses begins a sentence and the second clause "completes" the first, a comma should not separate the two clauses. If the second clause functions independently of the first, however, a comma should separate the two clauses.

## Chapter 2: Independent and Dependent Clauses

Consider the two sentences below:

- <u>Because Rick used a ladder</u> <u>that was old</u>, he had an unfortunate accident.
- <u>Although Ashley is saving a lot of money</u>, <u>unless her wages increase</u>, she will not be able to afford her dream car.

In the first sentence, *that was old* is a dependent clause that completes the first dependent clause, *Because Rick used a ladder*. Therefore, a comma is placed after the pair because the pair essentially functions as a single clause. In the second sentence, however, *unless her wages increase* does not complete the first dependent clause, *Although Ashley is saving a lot of money*. Consequently, a comma should separate the two independent clauses. (Concerning the second comma in the second sentence above, see Comma Rule #58 in chapter 8.)

Note that the structure of the second sentence above is awkward and can usually be avoided by switching the order of the last two clauses:

- Although Ashley is saving a lot of money, she will not be able to afford her dream car unless her wages increase.

# Chapter 3
# Introductory Elements

In chapter 2, you learned that commas are used after dependent clauses that begin sentences. In this chapter, you will learn about the other **introductory sentence elements** that should be followed by commas. Introductory elements are grammatical units that precede the traditional subject (including any subject descriptors) + verb sentence construction.

## 3.A: Adverbs

Recall from chapter 1 that **adverbs** are words that modify verbs, adjectives, or other adverbs. A great many adverbs end in the letters *ly* and relate to *manner*. In other words, they address the question of *how?* Note that adverbs of this nature usually modify verbs.

- He ran *quickly*. (*Quickly* describes how he *ran*.)
- She poured the drink *slowly*. (*Slowly* describes how she *poured*.)
- She danced *happily* across the stage. (*Happily* describes how she *danced*.)

> Comma Rule #8: A comma should follow an adverb that begins a sentence, modifies a verb, and is not followed immediately by the verb it modifies.

- *Jubilantly*, he received the championship trophy from the league director. (*Jubilantly* describes how he *received* the trophy.)
- *Reluctantly*, she drove to Washington to see her uncle. (*Reluctantly* describes how she *drove*.)

## Chapter 3: Introductory Elements

Adverbs of frequency are closely related to adverbs of manner because they address the question of *when* (similar to the question of *how*) and, consequently, modify verbs. These adverbs also take commas when they begin a sentence. Like adverbs of manner, adverbs of frequency end in the letters *ly* most of the time.

- *Occasionally,* you should change the oil in your car. (*Occasionally* describes how frequently you should *change* your car's oil.)

When an independent clause that follows a sentence-beginning *ly* adverb is short (seven words or fewer), the comma may be omitted. In fact, writers often take advantage of this exception to the rule. However, you will never be wrong to use the comma in such cases, and by doing so you will develop a good habit.

- *Periodically* they go dancing at the night club.
  or
- *Periodically,* they go dancing at the night club.

Some adverbs modify adjectives or other adverbs—not verbs. These adverbs are usually *not* followed by a comma when they begin a sentence.

- *Nearly* all Americans are familiar with at least one sport. (*Nearly* modifies *all*, which modifies *Americans* and is therefore an adjective in this sentence.)

- *Relatively* slow progress is being made on the construction project. (*Relatively* modifies *slow*, which modifies *progress* and is therefore an adjective in this sentence.)

Most of the time, adverbs of place and adverbs of direction do *not* need to be followed by a comma if they begin a sentence. Consider the following examples.

## Adverbs of Place

- *Afar* he went to find his special pair of shoes, but he could not find them.
- *Everywhere* he looked for his shoes, but he could not find them.

## Adverbs of Direction

- *Westward* they went in search of gold.
- *North* they drove as they sang the songs of the season.

If the verb that the adverb modifies *immediately* follows the sentence-beginning adverb, a comma should not be used.

- *Merrily* <u>went</u> Jack on his way.
- *Arrogantly* <u>did</u> the lawyer <u>lecture</u> the jury.

Such constructions are rare in modern writing, but you may encounter them occasionally.

Some adverbs reflect the attitude of the writer and modify the entire sentence, not just a word. Comma Rule #9 should be employed when such adverbs are placed at the beginning of a sentence.

---

Comma Rule #9: A comma should follow an adverb that begins a sentence and modifies the rest of the sentence.

---

- *Unfortunately*, seeing the movie was a waste of my time.
- *Apparently*, going to class is a requirement for getting a good grade.

Comma Rule #10 is about adverts of time, which include words such as *yesterday, today, before, afterwards,* etc.

---

Comma Rule #10: A comma *may* follow an adverb of time that begins a sentence.

---

As stated in Comma Rule #10, when adverbs of time begin sentences, they often should be followed by a comma. Because a comma indicates a short pause, and because a short pause may not always be desired after an adverb of time that begins a sentence, the decision to use a comma after this introductory element is really a matter of authorial preference. Authorial preference is especially relevant with adverbs of time that begin shorter sentences (approximately seven or fewer words). Writers should consider whether a pause would be desired after the adverb if the sentence were read aloud. Note, however, that you will never be wrong to use a comma after an adverb of time that begins a short sentence. When dealing with short sentences, you will usually want a comma after the adverb if the adverb itself is a word you wish to emphasize in the sentence.

- *Yesterday*, Joey and Ginger went to the retirement home to see their grandfather.
- *Afterwards*, the bartender served free drinks because he was so excited about the victory.
- *Today* he went to the store.
  or
- *Today*, he went to the store.

## 3.B: Transitional Expressions

Transitional expressions are words and phrases that connect ideas. They may connect paragraphs, sentences, or even ideas within in a sentence. Table 3.1 contains a list of common transitional words and expressions.

**Table 3.1**
**Common Transitional Expressions**

| above all | however | nevertheless |
|---|---|---|
| after all | in conclusion | nonetheless |
| again | in contrast | of course |
| also | indeed | on the contrary |
| as a matter of fact | in fact | on the one hand |
| as a result | in other words | on the other hand |
| consequently | instead | second |
| first | in the meantime | similarly |
| for example | likewise | therefore |
| for instance | meanwhile | third |
| furthermore | moreover | thus |
| hence | next | to summarize |

The list above is far from exhaustive. Many more transitional words are used in everyday speech and writing. These are just a few of the most common, but they should help you recognize transitional words and expressions when you see them.

> Comma Rule #11: A comma should follow a transitional word or expression that begins a sentence.

An exception to Comma Rule #11 is allowed for transitional words or expressions that begin short sentences (approximately seven or fewer words), but you will never be wrong to use a comma in such sentences. When a transitional expression begins a shorter sentence, consider whether you would want a pause after the transition if the sentence were read aloud.

- *On the one hand,* it is important to stay informed through the media.
- *On the other hand,* you cannot assume that everything you hear or read is true.

- *In the meantime,* he cleaned his room.
  or
- *In the meantime* he cleaned his room.

Many transitional expressions are called *conjunctive adverbs* (addressed in chapter 1) and are therefore subject to comma rules pertaining to adverbs as well. For instance, the word *next* is an adverb of time:

- The chef diced three onions. *Next,* he mixed the onions with salt and cabbage.

Some transitional words do not always function as transitions. When they do not, they probably do not need a comma.

- *First,* take the meat from the freezer and defrost it. *Second,* marinate the meat for at least six hours.
  but
- *First* place was awarded to the runner from Kansas City. *Second* place went to the competitor from southern Georgia.

In the first sentence above, the words *first* and *second* function as transitional words and, therefore, need commas. In the second sentence, the words function as adjectives—not as transitions—so they are not followed by commas.

## 3.C: Participles

Participles are words that *look* like verbs but function in sentences as adjectives. **Present participles** end in *-ing*. Examples of present participles include words such as *working, crying, jumping,* etc. While these words look like verbs, they cannot function alone as verbs. To be verbs, they would require helping verbs to be located alongside them.

- *was working*
- *is crying*

## Chapter 3: Introductory Elements

In the examples below, the italicized words are used as participles.

- The *working* television at the yard sale is worth more than the broken one beside it.
- The mother comforted her *crying* child.
- At the fair, the boy enjoyed the *jumping* frogs.

Care must be taken to distinguish present participles from **gerunds**. Gerunds also contain the letters *ing*, but gerunds function as nouns—not adjectives. Consider again the words *jumping* and *crying*. Whether such words are participles or gerunds is determined by their use in a sentence.

- *Jumping* is something Grandpa finds difficult in his old age. (*Jumping* is a gerund because it is used as a noun—the subject of the sentence.)
- *Jumping*, Jonathan made it over the puddle safely. (*Jumping* is a present participle because it is used as an adjective—it describes *Jonathan*.)
- *Crying* is something Jill does not tolerate. (*Crying* is a gerund because it is used as a noun—the subject of the sentence.)
- *Crying*, Jenny asked one more time for forgiveness. (*Crying* is a present participle because it is used as an adjective—it describes *Jenny*.)

**Past participles** usually end in *–ed*, though they may occasionally take an irregular form. Typical examples of past participles are *frustrated, annoyed, shamed*, etc. Examples of irregular past participles are *grown, ran,* and *thrown*. When such words are used as adjectives instead of verbs, they are past participles.

- Jerrod *frustrated* his teacher. (The word *frustrated* functions as a verb.)
- Jerrod's *frustrated* teacher decided to change the subject. (The word *frustrated* is a past participle because it functions as an adjective that describes *teacher*.)

- Sharon *annoyed* her big brother. (The word *annoyed* functions as a verb.)
- *Annoyed*, Sharon stomped out of the room. (The word *annoyed* is a past participle because it functions as an adjective that describes *Sharon*.)
- The tomatoes were *grown* on a farm near the river. (The word *grown* functions as a verb with the helping verb *were*.)
- The *grown* man no longer looks like the little boy he once was. (The word *grown* is a past participle because it functions as an adjective that describes *man*.)

Now that you can recognize participles, you are ready for Comma Rule #12.

Comma Rule #12: A comma should follow a present or past participle that begins a sentence and is not immediately followed by a dependent clause or a prepositional phrase.

- *Driving*, the man could not answer his cell phone in time.

- *Angered*, Sherry told her children to eat their food or go to their rooms.

Participles that are followed by prepositional phrases or dependent clauses begin **participial phrases**. A comma rule related to sentence-beginning participial phrases is presented later in this chapter.

# 3.D: Interjections

Recall from chapter 1 that **interjections** are words that indicate surprise or extreme emotion. Often, an interjection is followed by an exclamation point.

## Chapter 3: Introductory Elements

- *Hey!* You stepped on my toes!
- *Yikes!* That test was difficult!
- *Oh!* I didn't see you there.

Occasionally, an interjection that begins a sentence may be followed by a comma if an exclamation point is too strong for the sentence.

> Comma Rule #13: A comma should follow an interjection that begins a sentence and does not require an exclamation point.

- *Oh*, I did not realize I had cut in line.
- *Yes*, the check is in the mail.

## 3.E: Phrases

Recall from chapter 2 that a **phrase** is a group of words that does *not* contain both a subject and a verb. (A group of words that *does* contain both a subject and a verb is a clause.) There are various types of phrases. This part of the chapter addresses only phrases that should be followed by a comma when they begin a sentence.

**Prepositional Phrases**

Perhaps the most common and most used type of phrase is the prepositional phrase. Recall from chapter 1 that prepositional phrases begin with a preposition, end with a noun or pronoun (called the *object of the preposition*), and may or may not contain words that modify the noun or pronoun.

- *on the beach* (**on** [preposition] **the** [modifies *beach*] **beach** [noun/object of phrase])
- *in summer* (**in** [preposition] **summer** [noun/object of phrase])
- *above the blue sky* (**above** [preposition] **the** [modifies *sky*] **blue** [modifies *sky*] **sky** [noun/object of phrase])

- *with elegance* (**with** [preposition] **elegance** [noun/object of preposition])
- *in his deceitful way* (**in** [preposition] **his** [modifies *way*] **deceitful** [modifies *way*] **way** [noun/object of phrase])

You can easily recognize prepositional phrases if you can recognize prepositions, which always begin prepositional phrases. A preposition expresses relationship between a noun or a pronoun and other words. Some of the most common prepositions are listed in Table 3.2.

**Table 3.2**
**Common Prepositions**

| along | across | alongside |
|---|---|---|
| below | inside | in |
| beneath | of | for |
| behind | between | by |
| into | against | beside |
| off | beyond | among |
| onto | during | at |
| over | under | around |
| through | up | on |
| with | without | until |

Remember that many words can function as different parts of speech. *How* a word is used determines the part of speech it is in any given sentence. Most of the words in Table 3.2 are almost always used as prepositions. However, they *may* function as other parts of speech. The word *for*, for instance, is also one of the seven coordinating conjunctions.

Comma Rule #14: Generally, a comma should follow a prepositional phrase that begins a sentence and is not immediately followed by a dependent clause or a verb. If the subject of the verb is the "understood *you*," however, a comma should be placed between the prepositional phrase and the verb.

## Chapter 3: Introductory Elements

When a prepositional phrase begins a sentence, it should be followed by a comma unless the sentence is short and unless it is followed immediately by a verb or a dependent clause. When prepositional phrases begin shorter sentences, consider whether you would want a pause after the phrase if the sentence were read aloud. If a pause would be desired, then use a comma.

- *In the first quarter,* the quarterback completed seven passes.
- *With some hesitation,* Sally agreed to serve as a judge of the students' projects.
- *Until morning arrives,* she will sit by the window and wait on her son.
- *During the night,* the wind blew over the trees and caused electricity to go out in seven cities.
- *By day,* the boys behave. *At night,* they are rowdy.
  or
- *By day* the boys behave. *At night* they are rowdy.

Even when sentences are short, you should strongly consider using a comma after sentence-beginning prepositional phrases when phrases expresses clock or calendar time.

- *In July,* the board voted. (The prepositional phrase expresses calendar time.)
- *By Monday,* submit your resignation. (The prepositional phrase expresses calendar time.)
- *At seven p.m.,* the trumpet sounded. (The prepositional phrase expresses clock time.)

While a comma after the time-related phrases in the three examples above is not mandatory (because the sentences are very short), convention favors the comma. You will never be wrong to use a comma in the instances such as those demonstrated in the three sentences above.

If a verb immediately follows the sentence-beginning prepositional phrase, a comma should not be used—unless the subject of the verb is the "understood *you*." Note the difference between the two sentences below. In the first sentence, the subject is *collection*—the subject and verb are simply transposed so that the verb is placed immediately after the introductory prepositional phrase, *under the old maple tree*. However, in the second sentence, which expresses a command, an "invisible" subject—the "understood *you*"—is understood to be before the verb, so a comma should still be used after the prepositional phrase.

- *Under the old maple tree* <u>was</u> a valuable collection of fossils.
- *After the party,* <u>go</u> to the Lankfords' house to pick up your sister.

When working with sentence-beginning prepositional phrases, also be aware of Comma Rule #15.

---
Comma Rule #15: When consecutive prepositional phrases begin a sentence, a comma should follow the *final* phrase as long as it is not immediately followed by a dependent clause or a verb. If the subject of the verb is the "understood *you*," however, a comma should be placed between the final introductory phrase and the verb.

---

- <u>*In the middle of the night,*</u> Suzie awoke from a bad dream.
- <u>*Across the Delaware River toward the tavern by Washington's post,*</u> the troops gathered.

The two sentences above contain multiple introductory prepositional phrases that are followed by a comma. The first sentence below also contains a pair of introductory prepositional phrases—*in the middle* and *of the stream*—but a comma is *not* placed after these phrases because a verb immediately follows them.

- *In the middle of the stream* <u>was</u> a large trout.

The sentence below also contains more than one introductory prepositional phrase—*after the performance, at the end,* and *of the day*—and these phrases are also followed immediately by a verb. However, this sentence expresses a command and therefore contains an "invisible" subject—the "understood *you*." Consequently, a comma *is* used after the prepositional phrases.

- *After the performance at the end of the day,* <u>make</u> sure you clean the equipment.

If a dependent clause immediately follows a sentence-beginning prepositional phrase or group of phrases, a comma should be placed after the dependent clause instead of after the prepositional phrase.

- *Under an umbrella* <u>because the rain was falling hard</u>, Joey ran quickly to his car.

- *On fire* <u>until the rain fell</u>, the field's crops were destroyed.

**Participial Phrases**

As you have already learned from section 3.C of this chapter, participles are words that *look* like verbs but function in sentences as *adjectives*. Recall that present participles end in *–ing* (*banking, chopping, showing, telling,* etc.) While these words look like verbs, they cannot function alone as verbs. To be verbs, they would require helping verbs to be located alongside them.

- *was chopping*
- *is showing*

When helping verbs are absent and such words are used with other words as adjectives, they become **participial phrases.**

- *Betting on an easy victory,* the coach started his worst pitcher.
- *Showing a lot of compassion,* Jenny gave the stranded family a ride.

In the first sentence above, the italicized phrase describes *coach*. In the second sentence, the italicized phrase describes *Jenny*. Since *coach* and *Jenny* are both nouns, and since adjectives describe nouns, the italicized phrases are participial phrases because participial phrases function as adjectives.

As stated previously in this chapter, *past* participles usually end in *–ed*, though they may occasionally take an irregular form. Typical examples of past participles are *watched, hiked, annoyed,* etc. Examples of irregular past participles are *grown, ran,* and *thrown*. Like present participles and present participial phrases, past participles and past participial phrases look like verbs but function as adjectives.

- *Watched by the police,* Joshua was careful in his daily routine.
- Dr. Johnson paced the room, *annoyed that his guests were late.*
- *Grown on an organic farm,* the tomatoes that Julie served tasted better than the store-bought tomatoes that I usually buy.

In the examples above, the italicized phrases modify *Joshua, Dr. Johnson,* and *tomatoes*, respectively. Consequently, they function as adjectives and are therefore participial phrases.

Remember to distinguish present participial phrases from gerund phrases. Gerund phrases also contain *–ing* words, but gerunds function as nouns—not adjectives.

- *Chopping firewood* is stressful.
- *Showing horses* is his favorite thing to do.

In the sentences above, the italicized phrases function as sentence subjects. They are therefore nouns and, consequently, gerund phrases.

> Comma Rule #16: A comma should follow a participial phrase that begins a sentence.

- *Questioned about his involvement in the crime,* the man began to worry.
- *Helping whenever she sees an opportunity,* the woman is proving to be a wonderful asset to the firm.

## Chapter 3: Introductory Elements

- *Carrying on about his days as an athlete,* Richard is driving people away from the party.

For the purpose of Comma Rule #16, note that a prepositional phrase or a dependent clause usually completes a participial phrase and is therefore considered part of the participial phrase. In the first sentence above, for example, the prepositional phrases *about his involvement* and *in the crime* follow the past participle *questioned*. In the second sentence, the dependent clause *whenever she sees an opportunity* follows the present participle *helping*. In fact, any combination of prepositional phrases and dependent clauses may complete a participial phrase. In the examples below, the bolded dependent clauses have been added to the sentences from the examples above.

- *Questioned about his involvement in the crime* **because he was found so close to the scene**, the man began to worry.
- *Helping in various ways* **whenever she sees an opportunity**, the woman is proving to be a wonderful asset to the firm.
- *Carrying on about his days as an athlete* **as if people are interested in his stories**, Richard is driving people away from the party.

Treat such prepositional phrases and dependent clauses as part of one participial phrase until you reach the main subject or a sentence element that requires a comma before it because of another rule in this book.

**Infinitive Phrases**

Infinitive phrases also contain words that look like verbs but function as something else. They may function as nouns, adjectives, or adverbs, and they are almost always introduced by the word *to*.

- to live in Tokyo
- to eat
- to wrestle an alligator

## Chapter 3: Introductory Elements

> Comma Rule #17: A comma should follow an infinitive phrase that begins a sentence and functions as an adverb that describes a verb.

As Comma Rule #17 states, when an infinitive phrase begins a sentence and functions as an adverb that describes a verb, it should be followed by a comma. A sentence-beginning infinitive phrase used as a noun, however, needs no comma.

- *To win the contest,* you must practice for the next seven weeks. (The infinitive phrase is used as an adverb to describe why you *must practice,* so a comma is placed after the phrase.)
- *To win the contest* is to become the champion. (The infinitive phrase is used as the subject of the sentence—a noun phrase—so no comma is necessary.)

For the purpose of Comma Rule #17, note that a prepositional phrase or a dependent clause may complete an infinitive phrase. In such cases, a prepositional phrase or a dependent clause is considered part of the infinitive phrase. In fact, multiple prepositional phrases or dependent clauses, or a combination of the two, may complete an infinitive phrase.

- *To win the contest* **that you entered,** you must practice for the next seven weeks.
- *To win the contest* **in May,** you must practice for the next seven weeks.
- *To win the contest* **that you entered in March,** you must practice for the next seven weeks.

In the examples above, the infinitive phrases are italicized. In the first sentence, a dependent clause that is considered part of the infinitive phrase is bolded. In the second sentence, a prepositional phrase that is considered part of the infinitive phrase is bolded. In the third sentence, both a dependent clause *and* a prepositional phrase that are considered a part of the infinitive phrase are bolded. Treat prepositional phrases and dependent clauses as part of one infinitive phrase until you reach the main subject or a sentence element that requires a comma before it because of another rule in this book.

## Absolute Phrases

**Absolute phrases** sometimes look like participial phrases because they often have participles in them. However, they differ from participial phrases in the sense that they modify entire sentences instead of just one word.

- *Weather permitting,* the girls will go to the beach on Sunday.
- *The chores complete,* the boys entered the room with excitement about surprising their parents.

> Comma Rule #18: A comma should follow an absolute phrase that begins a sentence.

- *All things being equal,* the girls have a good shot at winning.
- *Rain pouring down on the roof,* the couple huddled inside by the fireplace during the storm.

# Chapter 4
# Mid-Sentence and End-of-Sentence Elements

Most of what you have learned so far has been about comma usage related to beginning-of-sentence elements. Mastering the rules of chapters 2 and 3 will help you effectively address approximately half of the comma-usage issues you will encounter in your writing. The remaining chapters address issues that are not necessarily governed by beginning-of-sentence rules.

In this chapter, you will learn about four mid-sentence and end-of-sentence elements that require commas when certain conditions are met. These elements are (1) nonrestrictive elements, (2) parenthetical expressions, (3) conjunctive adverbs and other transitional expressions, and (4) contrasting elements.

## 4.A: Nonrestrictive Elements

Some sentences contain **nonrestrictive** clauses, phrases, or words. Nonrestrictive elements are descriptive elements that do not restrict the meaning of a sentence. In other words, if a nonrestrictive element were removed from a given sentence, the sentence would still make sense. Consider the two sentences below.

- The purple car, *which gets great fuel mileage*, needs to be removed from the lawn.
- Emily's car, *parked haphazardly on the lawn*, needs to be towed to the garage for repairs.

The italicized word groups in the examples above are nonrestrictive elements because they do not affect the meaning of the sentences in which they are contained. In the first sentence, the fact that the car gets great fuel mileage has nothing to do with the fact that it needs to be removed from the lawn. Similarly, the phrase *parked haphazardly on the lawn* in the second sentence has nothing to do with the fact that Emily's car needs to be towed to the garage for repairs. In both sentences, readers would understand the meaning of the sentence if the nonrestrictive element were removed:

- The purple car needs to be removed from the lawn.
- Emily's car needs to be towed to the garage for repairs.

Many (not all) nonrestrictive elements are adjective clauses and begin with the relative pronouns *who* or *which*.

- Spring break, *which is usually in March*, is a time for stressed-out college students to relax after weeks of studying.
- Professor Smith, *who has three degrees*, will be reading to kindergarteners at the elementary school on Friday.

Nonrestrictive elements are actually central to the common question of when to use *which* and when to use *that*. The answer to this question is much simpler than many people realize: use *which* with nonrestrictive elements, and use *that* with **restrictive** elements, or elements that *do* restrict the meaning of a sentence.

- Jack's workshop, *which was built in 1942*, is in the southeast corner of his back yard.
- The workshop *that is in the southeast corner of Jack's back yard* is the one that needs the new roof.

In the first sentence above, the fact that Jack's workshop was built in 1942 does not affect the meaning of the sentence. In the second example, however, the reader assumes that Jack has more than one workshop, and only one of them—the one *that is in the southeast corner of Jack's back yard*—needs a new roof. The italicized clause in the second sentence is important—especially if the sentence is being communicated to the roofing company! In other words, the italicized clause in the second sentence is restrictive. It restricts the sentence's

## Chapter 4: Mid-Sentence and End-of-Sentence Elements

meaning. Because it is restrictive, it begins with *that*, not *which*—and it is not surrounded by commas.

Not all nonrestrictive elements begin with *which* or *who*, however. Many nonrestrictive elements are participial phrases. Recall from chapter 3 that participles are words that *look* like verbs but function in sentences as adjectives. Present participles end in *–ing* (*banking, chopping, showing, telling,* etc.). While these words look like verbs, they cannot function alone as verbs. To be verbs, they would require helping verbs to be located alongside them.

- *was chopping*
- *is showing*

As stated in the previous chapter, when helping verbs are absent and such words are used with other words as adjectives, they become participial phrases.

- *Banking on an easy victory,* the coach started his worst pitcher.
- *Showing a lot of compassion,* Jenny gave the stranded family a ride.

Past participles usually end in *–ed,* though they may occasionally take an irregular form. Examples of past participles that end in *–ed* are *watched, hiked, annoyed,* etc. Examples of irregular past participles are *grown, ran,* and *thrown.* Like present participles and present participial phrases, past participles and past participial phrases look like verbs but function as adjectives.

- *Watched by the police,* Joshua was careful in his daily routine.
- Dr. Johnson paced the room, *annoyed that his guests were late.*
- *Grown on an organic farm,* the tomatoes that Julie served tasted better than the store-bought tomatoes that I usually buy.

In the previous chapter, you learned that a past- or present-participial phrase should be followed by a comma when it begins a sentence. Notice, however, that a participial phrase can also be placed in the middle of a sentence.

- The coach, *banking on an easy victory*, started his worst players.
- Jenny, *showing a lot of compassion*, gave the stranded family a ride.
- Joshua, *watched by the police*, was careful in his daily routine.
- Dr. Johnson, *annoyed that his guests were late*, paced the room.
- Julie's tomatoes, *grown on an organic farm*, tasted better than the store-bought tomatoes that I usually buy.

While the italicized phrases in the examples above certainly *add* meaning to the sentences, they are nonrestrictive from a strictly grammatical perspective. That is, each sentence would still make sense if its participial phrase were omitted.

There is something else worth noticing about these examples. In every case, the word *who* or *which* (plus a helping verb) could be added to the beginning of the participial phrase.

- The coach, **who was** *banking on an easy victory*, started his worst pitcher.
- Jenny, **who was** *showing a lot of compassion*, gave the stranded family a ride.
- Joshua, **who was** *watched by the police*, was careful in his daily routine.
- Dr. Johnson, **who was** *annoyed that his guests were late*, paced the room.
- Julie's tomatoes, **which were** *grown on an organic farm*, tasted better than the store-bought tomatoes that I usually buy.

As a matter of fact, *who* or *which* (plus a helping verb) could be added to most other nonrestrictive elements as well.

- After the year 2001, **which was** *the year my first child was born*, fuel prices increased considerably.
- Dr. Fuller, **who is** *a Harvard graduate*, plays tennis on Saturdays.
- Mrs. Wilson, **who was** *at her wit's end*, disciplined her children sternly.
- The family dog, **which is** *twelve years old*, sleeps in the garage.

## Chapter 4: Mid-Sentence and End-of-Sentence Elements

(Coincidentally, all of these examples demonstrate another simple rule that is good to know. *Who* is used when referring to people; *which* and *that* are used when referring to all other nouns, living or nonliving.)

> Comma Rule #19: Commas should be placed around a nonrestrictive element that occurs in the middle of a sentence, and a comma should precede a nonrestrictive element that occurs at the end of a sentence.

In the examples from this section, you have probably noticed that commas are placed *on both sides* of a nonrestrictive element in the middle of a sentence. Placing commas on both sides of a nonrestrictive element signals to your reader that the information contained within the commas is not essential; it is simply extra information that adds color to your sentence.

As stated in Comma Rule #19, a comma must also set off a nonrestrictive element that occurs at the end of a sentence.

- Dr. Fuller attended Harvard College, *which has been around for over three hundred years.*
- Carlos married Juanita, *who was born in Canada.*
- Taryn placed her muddy shoes on the couch, *which was purchased at the local furniture store.*

Note that Comma Rule #19 governs comma usage related to an issue that confuses many writers: whether to use commas around names that serve as appositives. An **appositive** is a word, phrase, or clause that renames a noun or pronoun that has appeared before it, and comma usage related to appositives is often incorrect in American writing. Many people *always* use a comma with a name that serves as an appositive, but a comma is not always needed. Consider the two sentences below.

- My sister Rachel is older than my sister Angie.
- The team's captain, Casey Wentworth, was the only player who performed well yesterday.

In the first sentence, *Rachel* and *Angie* are restrictive words. The sentence would not make sense if the names were removed (*My sister is older than my sister*), so they do not need commas around them. In the second sentence, *Casey Wentworth* is a nonrestrictive name. If the name were removed, the sentence would still make sense. In short, Comma Rule #19 applies to names used as appositives as well as to other elements.

Note, however, that writers may or may not wish to treat names as appositives, and their punctuation will determine how they wish sentences to be read or spoken. Consider the two sentences below.

- Director of Online Education, Lisa Albauch, says that even small children are now taking courses online.
- Director of Online Education Lisa Albauch says that even small children are now taking courses online.

In the first sentence above, the writer wishes the emphasis to be on the title *Director of Online Education* and wishes to treat the name *Lisa Albauch* as an appositive. That is, the name simply *renames* the phrase *Director of Online Education*. Therefore, commas signal short pauses before and after the name. In the second sentence, however, the name serves as a noun that is *described* by the phrase *Director of Online Education*. In other words, the phrase at the beginning functions more like an adjective, and no pause would occur if the name were read aloud. Authorial preference should govern comma usage in such cases as those demonstrated above. If the writer wishes that the name *rename* a previous word or phrase, then the name should be treated as an appositive and a comma should be used. If, however, the writer wishes the name to be the *receiver of description* embodied by a previous word or phrase, then the name is not an appositive and commas should be omitted.

## 4.B: Parenthetical Expressions

Another element that requires comma usage with it is a **parenthetical expression.** A parenthetical expression is, technically, a

## Chapter 4: Mid-Sentence and End-of-Sentence Elements

type of nonrestrictive element. It is categorized separately only because it does not describe anything else in a sentence, whereas the nonrestrictive elements already addressed in this chapter describe other words.

In writing, *parenthetical* information is secondary to the main point. It interrupts the flow of thought in a sentence in order to communicate a digression. You have probably read something in which *parentheses* were used to set off such information. Often (but not always), information enclosed in parentheses represents an entirely separate, *free-standing* grammatical thought that does not flow with the rest of the sentence. Consider the two examples below.

- Our camping trip to Utah (Oh, the fun we had!) was the last trip I took with my father.
- My grandpa always said that traveling with my family (I had seven siblings) was like trying to herd cats.

When the parenthetical information represents a free-standing grammatical structure on its own, as in the examples above, parentheses or dashes should always be used to set off the information. Sometimes, however, the parenthetical information does not constitute a *free-standing grammatical thought*; rather, it simply interrupts a main thought with a word, phrase, or clause that could not stand alone. In these cases, writers have a choice of which punctuation to use—commas, parentheses, or dashes. Generally, parentheses and dashes are reserved for stronger interruptions; commas should be used when the information is only minimally interruptive.

---

Comma Rule #20: Commas should be placed around a minimally interruptive parenthetical expression that occurs in the middle of a sentence, and a comma should precede a minimally interruptive parenthetical expression that occurs at the end of a sentence.

---

- The movie's sequel, *according to the local teenagers who recently went to see it*, is not as technologically innovative as the original.

- The Grand Canyon, *some say*, was once used as a giant fortress for Native Americans.
- My brother's new book is not worth the paper it is printed on, *in one critic's opinion*.
- The woman's recovery, *we all hope*, will be a speedy one.
- His story was less than convincing, *to tell the truth*.

## 4.C: Conjunctive Adverbs and Other Transitional Expressions

In the previous chapter, you learned that transitional expressions, including conjunctive adverbs such as *furthermore, consequently, meanwhile*, etc., should be followed by a comma when they begin a sentence. (Table 3.1 in chapter 3 contains a list of common transitional expressions.) These words and phrases can also appear in the middle of or at the end of a sentence.

> Comma Rule #21: Commas should be placed around a conjunctive adverb or other transitional expression that occurs in the middle of a sentence and *precedes* the main verb, and a comma should precede a conjunctive adverb or other transitional expression that occurs at the end of a sentence.

When we speak a sentence with a transitional expression in the middle or at the end of it, we usually pause briefly to communicate the transition. Because the comma indicates a brief pause, transitional expressions should usually be surrounded by commas when they are written in a sentence, especially if they precede the main verb.

- The mouse fell for the trap. The rat, *however,* <u>was</u> too smart.
- The job's salary would be nice. The long hours, *on the other hand,* <u>are</u> not so desirable.
- Little Bobby hated the grocery store, and his sister, *similarly,* <u>detested</u> the Post Office.

## Chapter 4: Mid-Sentence and End-of-Sentence Elements

- Professional athletes in the major sports participate in long seasons. Baseball players play from April through September, *for example.*

In the examples immediately above, the transitional expressions that occur in the middle of a sentence are placed between a subject and a verb. Transitional expressions in the middle of a sentence may also appear *after* a verb, however. English language purists argue that a writer should not "split" a verb phrase with an adverb, as in the sentence, *I am, consequently, eating the popcorn,* where *am* is a helping verb for *eating.* However, people frequently split verb phrases in speech, so it is overly pedantic to cling to such an antiquated practice. Therefore, it is good to be aware of Comma rule #22:

> Comma Rule #22: Commas may or may not be placed around a mid-sentence conjunctive adverb or other transitional expression that occurs immediately after a verb. In most such cases, the decision to set off the transitional expression with commas—either after a linking verb, helping verb, action verb, or after an entire verb phrase—is a matter of the writer's taste.

If the writer would pause at the expression when speaking the sentence, then he or she should use commas.

- The mouse ingested the poison. It is, *therefore,* dead.

However, if the writer would not pause at the transitional expression when speaking the sentence, then he or she should not use commas.

- The mouse ingested the poison. It is *therefore* dead.

Either of the above approaches might be appropriate at any given time for any given writer. Both approaches can be encountered in much writing and in everyday conversation. The most important thing to recognize is that this exception applies only if a transitional

Chapter 4: Mid-Sentence and End-of-Sentence Elements

expression occurs *immediately* after a verb. (Note from the two examples above that a pause—represented by the commas—is usually marked by a drop in voice tone in native English speakers.)

Writers should observe a special rule regarding the word *however* when it is used as a transitional expression. That is, when used in the middle of a sentence, *however* must *always* have punctuation on both sides of it, even if it occurs immediately after a verb.

- Jeremy thought he played a good game. His coach, *however*, saw things differently. (*however* used as a mid-sentence transitional expression between a subject and a verb and surrounded by commas)
- Jeremy did not receive the Most Valuable Player Award. He did, *however*, receive the scholarship he wanted. (*however* used as a mid-sentence transitional expression between a helping verb and action verb and surrounded by commas)

When *however* is used to join two independent clauses, the punctuation on its left side should be a semicolon (if the two thoughts are closely connected) or a period. Only a coordinating conjunction (*and, but, or, nor, for, so, yet*—see chapter 2) may join two independent clauses with the assistance of a comma.

- *Incorrect*: Jeremy played a good game, *however*, his coach yelled at him anyway. (The word *however* cannot join the two independent clauses with a comma because it is not one of the seven coordinating conjunctions. It requires stronger punctuation to its left.)
- Correct: Jeremy played a good game. *However*, his coach yelled at him anyway.
- Correct: Jeremy scored forty points; *however*, his team lost anyway.

(Note: When used as transitional expression, the word *however* is a substitute for words and phrases such as *nevertheless, on the other hand, in spite of,* etc. It should not be confused with its subordinating conjunction form meaning "no matter how," as in the sentence,

*However you choose to repair the car, please repair it soon.* Commas are *not* used with the word *however* when it is used as a subordinating conjunction.)

## 4.D: Contrasting Elements

A contrasting element is a type of transitional expression. Like all transitional expressions, contrasting elements bridge two thoughts. Specifically, words and phrases of contrast demonstrate the *difference* between two trains of thought. Table 4.1 contains a few of the most common contrasting elements.

**Table 4.1**
**Common Expressions of Contrast**

| on the other hand | on the contrary | not |
|---|---|---|
| opposed to… | different from/than… | more than… |
| better than… | less than… | opposite… |
| unlike… | instead of… | though/while not… |

Be aware that the words and phrases in Table 4.1 are not always used as contrasting elements. When they are not used as contrasting elements, they might not need commas, so care must be taken to correctly determine their usage.

- Gregory's truck is *not* like Michael's.
  but
- Gregory's truck, *not Michael's*, won the show.


- Cassie was *opposed to* going to Europe.
  but
- Cassie, *opposed to Elizabeth*, went to Europe.

---
Comma Rule #23: Commas should be placed around a contrasting element that occurs in the middle of a sentence, and a comma should precede a contrasting element that occurs at the end of a sentence.
---

## Chapter 4: Mid-Sentence and End-of-Sentence Elements

- Curling, *unlike bowling*, is played on ice.
- The meal was charged to Paul's credit card, *not Barbara's*.

# Chapter 5
# Standard Serial Items and Coordinate Adjectives

This chapter addresses the comma rules for items in a series, or serial items. It is divided into two parts: a section about serial items and a section about coordinate adjectives. Coordinate adjectives are actually quasi-serial items, but a special rule applies to these elements. Therefore, they are addressed separately.

## 5.A: Standard Serial Items

When a sentence contains only *two* words, phrases, or clauses that go together, they should be separated by just the word *and* (or occasionally the word *or*).

- *Linda and Jerry* attended the matinee together. (two words used as subjects)
- *Allie or Jenny* should clean up the mess. (two words used as subjects)
- Joseph *ran and stretched* to prepare for the day's game. (two words used as verbs)
- While he was camping, Brett cooked *hamburgers and steaks*. (two words used as direct objects)
- The *red and yellow* chair was almost ruined. (two words used as adjectives)
- Linda played *by the pool and on the lawn* as she waited for her father. (two adverbial prepositional phrases)
- When Samson's mother returned home, she discovered *that Josie had made a mess on the floor and that Danielle had broken a window.* (two dependent clauses)

## Chapter 5: Standard Serial Items and Coordinate Adjectives

In grammatical terms, a **series** is simply a group of *three or more* words, phrases, or clauses that appear together within a sentence. Serial items must be separated by commas, and the word *and* (or occasionally the word *or*) should appear between the last two items.

> Comma Rule #24: Commas should be used to separate all of the items in a series of like elements, and the coordinating conjunction *and* or *or* should be placed after the comma that separates the last and second-to-last items.

- *Linda, Jerry, and Joseph* attended the matinee together. (three words used as subjects)
- *Allie, Jenny, or Lauren* should clean up the mess. (three words used as subjects)
- Joseph *ran, jogged, walked, and stretched* to prepare for the day's game. (four words used as verbs)
- While he was camping, Brett cooked *hamburgers, potatoes, and steaks*. (three words used as direct objects)
- The *red, green, and gold* chair was almost ruined. (three words used as adjectives)
- Lydia played *by the pool, under the tree, and on the lawn* as she waited for her father. (three adverbial prepositional phrases)
- When Samson's mother returned home, she discovered *that Josie had made a mess on the floor, that Danielle had broken a window, and that Missy had fed the dog too much food*. (three dependent clauses)

Note that a comma is not placed before the initial item or after the final item in a series unless one is required because of another comma rule.

- *Hiking, biking, and running* are three of my favorite activities. (A comma is not needed after *running*.)
- *Hiking, biking, and running*, all of which require much energy, are three of my favorite activities. (A comma is used after *running* because a nonrestrictive element follows.)

Chapter 5: Standard Serial Items and Coordinate Adjectives

In recent years, for no apparent reason except to save the amount of space that a comma occupies in a sentence, the practice of omitting the final comma (the one between the last two items in a series) has become common, especially in journalistic writing. The omission of the final comma in a series can cause confusion, however. Consider the sentences below.

- *Confusing*: There were different colors of chairs in the room: brown, yellow, pink and black. (Did some chairs have both pink and black material on them, or were there four different styles of chairs?)
- *Clear*: There were different colors of chairs in the room: brown, yellow, pink, and black.
- *Confusing*: The award recipient thanked his teachers, John and Sheila. (Are John and Sheila the names of the award recipient's teachers (appositives), or are they people who were thanked in addition to the teachers?)
- *Clear*: The award recipient thanked his teachers, John, and Sheila. (if John and Sheila are not meant to be appositives)

To avoid potentially confusing sentences, you should always insert a comma between the last two items in a series (before the coordinating conjunction *and* or *or* that joins the final two items). You will never be wrong to do so.

## 5.B: Coordinate Adjectives

Recall from chapter 1 that adjectives are words that describe nouns or pronouns.

- *blue* car
- *wild* hog
- *beautiful* sunset
- *thirsty* boy

## Chapter 5: Standard Serial Items and Coordinate Adjectives

When two or more adjectives "equally" describe the same noun(s) or pronoun(s), they are called **coordinate adjectives**. A special rule applies to the punctuation of coordinate adjectives. That is, a comma or commas may be used *without* a coordinating conjunction to separate a pair or a series of coordinate adjectives.

> Comma Rule #25: Commas should separate coordinate adjectives that precede the nouns or pronouns they modify, and the use of the coordinating conjunction *and* or *or* between either a pair of coordinate adjectives or between the last two items in a series of coordinate adjectives is a matter of authorial preference.

- Johnson tried to avoid the *smoky, dingy* bar.
- The *rickety, dangerous* elevator frightened all who looked upon it.
- *Windy, slick* roads should be avoided, especially at night.

The coordinating conjunctions *and* or *or* may or may not be used between a pair of coordinate adjectives or between the final comma and the final adjective in a series of coordinate adjectives. The decision to use the word **and** or **or** with coordinate adjectives is a matter of each writer's taste. In some cases, using a coordinating conjunction might make the sentence awkward. In other cases, it is perfectly acceptable.

- Johnson tried to avoid the *smoky, dingy, greasy* bar.
- The *tall, rickety,* **and** *dangerous* elevator frightened all who looked upon it.
- *Slick, windy, narrow* roads should be avoided, especially at night.

Regarding the punctuation of *two* coordinate adjectives, note that a comma may be used instead of *and* or *or* only when the coordinate adjectives *precede* the noun(s) or pronoun(s) they describe, not when they *follow* the noun(s) or pronoun(s) they describe.

## Chapter 5: Standard Serial Items and Coordinate Adjectives

- Johnson tried to avoid the *smoky, dingy* bar.

or

- Johnson tried to avoid the bar that was *smoky and dingy*.

but not

- Johnson tried to avoid the bar that was ~~*smoky, dingy*~~.

Care must be taken to distinguish coordinate adjectives from multiple adjectives that simply appear beside each other and are *not* coordinate. In order to be coordinate adjectives, the adjectives must relate equally to the noun(s) or pronoun(s) they describe.

A couple of simple tests can determine if adjectives are coordinate adjectives. One test involves inserting the word *and* between the adjectives. If the sentence still makes sense with the word *and* inserted, then the adjectives are coordinate adjectives.

- *Coordinate Adjectives*: The *dark, stormy* night terrified the children. (This sentence would still make sense if the word *and* were inserted, so *dark* and *stormy* are coordinate adjectives.)
- *Not Coordinate Adjectives*: I grew up in a *yellow farm* house in Nebraska. (This sentence would not make sense if the word *and* were inserted, so *yellow* and *farm* are not coordinate adjectives.)

The other test involves reversing the order of the adjectives. If the sentence still makes sense when the order of the adjectives is reversed, then the adjectives are coordinate adjectives.

- *Coordinate Adjectives*: The *beautiful, healthy* baby looked up at his mother from his crib. (This sentence would still make sense if the order of the words *beautiful* and *healthy* were reversed: The *healthy, beautiful* baby looked up at his mother from his crib.)
- *Not Coordinate Adjectives*: My sister is a *talented union* mason. (This sentence would not make sense if the order of the words *talented* and *union* were reversed: My sister is a ~~*union talented*~~ mason.)

Recall from chapter 1 that many adjectives can also function as nouns. For instance, in the sentence, *Jacilyn went on a spending spree*, the word *spending* is an adjective. In the sentence, *I am better at spending than at saving,* the word *spending* is a noun that functions as the object of the preposition *at*.

Also note that care must be taken to distinguish adjectives from adverbs. Consider the sentences below.

- Shelby ran *fast* in yesterday's race. (The word *fast* is an adverb because it describes ran, which is a verb.)
- Shelby is a *fast* runner. (The word *fast* is an adjective because it describes *runner*, which is a noun.)

# Chapter 6
# Quotations and Dialogue, Direct Address, and Tag Questions

This chapter addresses a few additional sentence elements that interrupt the flow of a sentence and therefore require commas. These elements are quotations and dialogue, direct address, and tag questions. Definitions of these elements are provided as they are introduced in the chapter. Many of the rules in this chapter are long and detailed, so you will benefit from studying the examples carefully.

## 6.A: Quotations and Dialogue

Quotations are, of course, words and phrases that are attributed to someone other than the author who is incorporating them into a sentence. Writers place quotation marks around quoted material to signal that the words they are quoting are not their own. In nonfiction, writers use quotation marks to avoid plagiarism. In fiction, quotation marks are used to separate a character's speech from the author's narration. The process of characters communicating with each other is called dialogue. For the remainder of this chapter, the word *quotation* will refer to both quotations and dialogue, for comma rules are the same for both.

While quotation marks are important, they are not the only marks of punctuation that are used with quotations. Commas are also used with quoted information, and their function is an important one.

Chapter 6: Quotations and Dialogue, Direct Address, and Tag Questions

## Quotations That Follow Explanatory Information and End a Sentence

> Comma Rule #26: When a quotation that ends a sentence follows a phrase such as *according to* or *as [someone] puts it*, or explanatory information containing the word *said* or one of its substitutes, and when the quotation does not blend with the grammatical structure of the sentence, a comma should be placed immediately after the explanatory information that precedes the quotation.

Probably the most common way to use a quotation in a sentence is to use explanatory information and the word *said* or one of its substitutes *before* the quotation.

- John *said*, "Get back to your room!"
- After he ate dinner, Uncle Joe relaxed in his chair and *exclaimed*, "That was the best steak I've ever had!"
- Speaking to a large audience, the guest speaker *cautioned*, "We should all stop worrying about things we cannot control."
- The president *declared* in response to the offense, "A new curfew will be imposed across town." (Note that the quotation does not need to start *immediately* after *said* or one of its substitutes. In this sentence, for example, the prepositional phrases *in response* and *to the offense* follow the verb *declared*. When additional explanatory information follows the verb, the comma is placed at the end of the explanatory information.)

Each sentence above contains a verb that introduces the quotation. In the first sentence, the introductory verb is *said*, which is the most common introductory verb. *Exclaimed* introduces the quotation in the second sentence, and *cautioned* introduces the quotation in the third sentence. Notice that a comma is placed immediately after the explanatory information. Also notice that the punctuation at the end of a quotation is the final punctuation if the quotation ends the sentence.

Chapter 6: Quotations and Dialogue, Direct Address, and Tag Questions

Table 6.1 contains a few substitutes for the word *said*. Other substitutes for *said* may be found in Victor C. Pellegrino's excellent little book titled *A Writer's Guide to Transitional Words and Expressions*.

**Table 6.1**
**Common Substitutes for the Word *Said***

| addressed | asked     | answered  | argued     | bragged   |
|-----------|-----------|-----------|------------|-----------|
| claimed   | confessed | confirmed | criticized | declared  |
| explained | groaned   | insisted  | jeered     | maintained|
| mocked    | noted     | opined    | pointed out| pleaded   |
| prayed    | replied   | stated    | suggested  | wrote     |

- The waiter *asked*, "Would you prefer a booth or a table?"
- The customer *answered*, "I would prefer a booth."
- After his last victory, Joey *bragged*, "I have won four tournaments in a row!"
- The boy *confessed* to his father, "I broke the window with my baseball."
- When Lucy fell down, the other girls *jeered*, "Lucy is clumsy."
- As Mr. Jackson *noted* in his speech, "Political games are no fun for those who lose them."
- At church the woman *prayed*, "Please allow me to live another day."
- In chapter 4 the author *writes*, "She waited for the water to wash her weary eyes."

Notice that the quotations in the examples above do not blend with the grammatical structure of the sentences in which they are contained. Rather, they are grammatical structures all their own.

When a quotation *does* blend with the grammatical structure of the sentence, a comma should *not* precede it. Often, a quotation can be blended with the grammatical structure of a sentence by simply placing the word *that* before it.

- Lori said *that* "being a mother is wonderful."

- The doctor says *that* "snoring can cause problems in a marriage."

In both of the examples above, the relative pronoun *that* changes the dynamic of the sentence so that a dependent noun clause functions as the direct object. If the word *that* were omitted, a comma would be used.

- Lori said, "Being a mother is wonderful."
- The doctor says, "Snoring can cause problems in a marriage."

*That* is probably the most common word that allows a quotation to fit grammatically with the rest of a sentence, but other words may be used similarly.

- James asserted that the team won the game *by* "playing hard and making good decisions."
- According to Mr. Richter, the trip went *as* "smoothly as it could have gone."
- Jane said she would return *in* "just a minute."

Sometimes a verb that appears immediately before a quotation is *not* a substitute for the word *said*. In such cases, no comma is used.

- According to Mr. Richter, the trip *went* "as smoothly as it could have gone."
- Blake said that we should *play* "as if it is our last game."

In the sentences above, *went* and *play* are not substitutes for the word *said*. While the quotation marks indicate that *as smoothly as it could have gone* and *as if it is our last game* are Mr. Richter's and Blake's exact words, neither quotation is set off with a comma. *Went* and *play* simply allow the quotation to blend grammatically with the rest of the sentence.

Note that the first word of a quotation that follows a comma is capitalized. This is because such quotations are usually complete sentences in and of themselves. Coincidentally, this is also why they do not blend grammatically with the rest of a sentence. A quotation that is not preceded by a comma is not capitalized because it functions as a grammatical continuation of previous sentence elements.

Sometimes, quotations are introduced with a phrase such as *according to* or a clause such as *as [someone] puts it*. Although such phrases and clauses do not contain the word *said* or one of its substitutes, the phrases and the explanatory information that accompanies them requires a comma when the quotation does not blend with the grammatical structure of the sentence.

- According to Dr. James Hill, "Fewer birds have migrated south in recent years."
- As local reporter Seymour Griffin puts it, "The hurricane is the worst that the coast has seen in eighty years."

Note that, technically, phrases such as "according to" are also governed by Comma Rule #14 from chapter 3, which reads as follows: "*Generally*, a comma should follow a prepositional phrase that begins a sentence and is not immediately followed by a dependent clause or a verb." Similarly, the clause "as [someone] puts it" is governed by Comma Rule #4 from chapter 2: "*Generally*, a comma should follow a dependent clause that begins with a subordinating conjunction and is followed by an independent clause."

## Quotations That Begin a Sentence and Are Followed by Explanatory Information

Quotations may also appear at the beginning of a sentence—*before* the explanatory information. A rule similar to Comma Rule #26 guides comma usage for such instances.

Chapter 6: Quotations and Dialogue, Direct Address, and Tag Questions

> Comma Rule #27: When a quotation begins a sentence and is followed by a phrase such as *according to* or *as [someone] puts it*, or explanatory information containing the word *said* or one of its substitutes, and when the quotation does not blend with the grammatical structure of the sentence, a comma should be placed immediately before the closing quotation marks.

- "We need a bigger house," Suzie said as her sister put away her clothes.
- "I hope it snows tomorrow," Johnny said as he stared with excitement at his new sled.

Note that the same qualifications that are stated in Comma Rule #26 are also stated in Comma Rule #27. That is, when a sentence-beginning quotation blends with the grammatical structure of the rest of a sentence, a comma is not used with the quotation. Observe, however, that such constructions are uncommon. Usually, such constructions reference quotations as quotations.

- "There is nothing new under the sun" is a quotation from the Bible.
- "The grass is greener on the other side" is a saying that has been around for many years.

When a question mark or an exclamation point is used at the end of a quotation that begins a sentence, no comma is used between the quotation and the explanatory information that follows.

- "We won!" the boys shouted to their mother when they walked through the front door.
- "Are we there yet?" the little girl asked her father.

**Quotations That Occur in the Middle of a Sentence**

Sometimes, quotations have explanatory information both before and after them. In such cases, observe Comma Rule #28.

Chapter 6: Quotations and Dialogue, Direct Address, and Tag Questions

> Comma Rule #28: When a quotation occurs in the middle of a sentence and is either preceded by or followed by a phrase such as *according to* or *as [someone] puts it*, or explanatory information containing the word *said* or one of its substitutes, and when the quotation does not blend with the grammatical structure of the sentence, a comma should be placed immediately after the explanatory information to its left and immediately before its closing quotation marks.

- Ian warned, "Those clouds are moving toward us," but the group was caught in the storm anyway.
- After the game, the coach told his players, "I am very proud of you," and many of the girls cried.
- The rancher said to the farmer, "I've tried everything I know to keep my livestock out of your field," yet the rancher's cows continued to ruin the farmer's corn.

When a question mark or an exclamation point is used at the end of a quotation that occurs in the middle of a sentence, no comma is needed before the closing quotation marks.

- The boys shouted, "We won!" and then they danced around the table.
- When traveling, the little girl often asked, "Are we there yet?" and her father would laugh every time he heard the question.

When one of the qualifications in Comma Rule #28 is not met, another rule may necessitate a comma on one side of the quotation or the other. Consider the following examples.

- When Elizabeth said that "alligators have been within twenty feet of the house," I decided that I did not want to play outside any longer. (In this sentence, no comma is placed before the quotation because the word *that* precedes the quotation and thus allows it to fit the grammatical structure of the sentence. A comma is placed at the end of the quotation, however, because

the quotation completes a dependent clause that begins a sentence. See Comma Rule #4 from chapter 2.)
- Of all the Shakespearean lines in my book, "To be or not to be" is the easiest for me to remember. (In this sentence, no comma is used at the end of the quotation because the quotation fits the grammatical structure of the latter part of the sentence. It is not followed by the word *said* or one of its substitutes, and the quotation itself is used as a single grammatical element (the subject of an independent clause. A comma precedes the quotation, however, because of Comma Rule #14 from chapter 3, which reads as follows: "Generally, a comma should follow a prepositional phrase that begins a sentence and is not immediately followed by a dependent clause or a verb."
- Georgia told her sister to "turn the horrible music down," but her sister refused to listen. (The use of the word *to* in this example allows the quotation to continue the grammatical structure of the sentence; therefore, no comma is placed before the quotation. Precisely because it continues the grammatical structure of the sentence, however, it completes an independent clause that begins with the words *Georgia told her sister to*, and Comma Rule #1 from chapter 2 states that "a sentence comprised of two independent clauses or complete thoughts should be joined by both a comma and a coordinating conjunction, and the comma should be placed before the conjunction." Since *her sister refused to listen* is also an independent clause, Comma Rule #1 applies.)

**Quotations That Are Broken by Explanatory Information**

Comma Rule #29: When a quotation is broken by a phrase such as *according to* or *as [someone] puts it*, or explanatory information containing the word *said* or one of its substitutes, a comma should be placed immediately before the closing quotation marks in the first part of the quotation and immediately after the explanatory information that precedes the second part of the quotation.

- "This restaurant's salsa," said the waiter, "is the best in the city."
- "When summer arrives," declared Melissa, "the beach will be my home."
- "I'm tired," complained the small child to his mother, "but I don't want to go home yet."
- "Get out of my room," the girl shouted to her little brother, "and don't come back!"

Note in the sentences above that the first word in the second part of a quotation (*is*, *the*, *but*, and *and*) is not capitalized because the second part of the quotation is simply a continuation of the first part. If the second part of the quotation began a new sentence, as in the example below, then the first word of the second part would be capitalized.

- "This trip is taking too long," complained Melissa. "When will we get there?"

In each of the examples immediately below Comma Rule #29, the second part of the quotation ends the sentence, so the punctuation that ends the quotation also serves as the punctuation that ends the entire sentence. When non-quoted information appears after the second part of the quotation, Comma Rule #28 from this chapter may be relevant as well. In other words, a comma might need to be placed inside the quotation marks that close the second part of the quotation.

- "I'm tired," complained the small child to his mother, "and I want to go home," so the mother began to rush.

## 6.B: Direct Address

Direct address occurs when the person or group being spoken to (or written to) is addressed by name. Listed below are three comma rules related to direct address. Examples are given with each rule.

Chapter 6: Quotations and Dialogue, Direct Address, and Tag Questions

> Comma Rule #30: A comma should be placed immediately after direct address that begins a sentence.

- *Friends,* I have some good news.
- *Ladies and gentlemen,* the program will begin in five minutes.
- *Robert, Leroy,* and *Dillon,* please pass your papers to the front of the room.

> Comma Rule #31: Commas should surround direct address that occurs in the middle of a sentence.

- The food, *folks,* is in the refrigerator.
- Your meatloaf, *Mom,* was delicious.

(These examples demonstrate an uncommon sentence construction that should usually be avoided.)

> Comma Rule #32: A comma should precede direct address that ends a sentence.

- Do you know where we are going, *Sherry*?
- How far before we reach the other side, *Bill*?

## 6.C: Tag Questions

A tag question is a short question that is almost always placed at the end of a sentence. Generally, a tag question seeks to confirm what has already been stated in the sentence. Tag questions are easy to recognize. They are italicized in the sentences below Comma Rule #33.

> Comma Rule #33: A comma should precede a tag question that occurs at the end of a sentence.

- We are not going to the play tonight, *are we*?
- The bill is on the table, *right*?

Chapter 6: Quotations and Dialogue, Direct Address, and Tag Questions

- I agree with Debbie, *don't you*?
- That dress is beautiful, *isn't it*?

Occasionally, a tag question may be placed in the middle of a sentence.

---
Comma Rule #34: Commas should be placed around a tag question that occurs in the middle of a sentence.
---

- The game will go faster, *won't it*, if we allow only two strikes instead of three?

Note that such a construction as the one above is usually awkward and should be avoided if possible. Also note that the question mark is placed at the end of the sentence, not immediately after the tag question.

# Chapter 7
# Dates, Addresses and City/State Locations, Titles and Designations, Numbers, and Correspondence

If you have a good grasp of the comma rules presented in chapters 2–6, you should be prepared to use commas properly in much of your writing. The issues addressed in this chapter are probably not *as* common as the issues addressed in the first chapters, but they are not uncommon, either. You will certainly benefit from knowing the comma rules that govern the use of dates, addresses, titles and designations, numbers, and correspondence.

## 7.A: Dates

The most acceptable style for writing dates is the month-day-year style, in which "day" refers to a numerical calendar day, not a day of the week. The month-day-year style is the style that is recommended in *The Chicago Manual of Style*, which is the most authoritative reference book on English language usage. This is also the style to which most people are accustomed.

- Hattie was born on July 6, 1933.
- The centennial celebration is scheduled for October 15, 2012.

Of course, a day of the week may be used in the month-day-year style for writing dates. It simply comes first, before the month. Often, the year is absent when a weekday is used, as in the third example below Comma Rule #35.

Chapter 7: Dates, Addresses and City/State Locations, Titles and Designations, Numbers, and Correspondence

> Comma Rule #35: In the month-day-year style for writing dates, commas are placed between the calendar day and the year and between the weekday and the month, if a weekday is used.

- Hattie was born on Friday, July 6, 1933.
- The centennial celebration is scheduled for Wednesday, October 15, 2012.
- I have to see the dentist on Monday, June 3.

Sometimes, a date written in the month-day-year style is placed at the beginning of or in the middle of a sentence.

> Comma Rule #36: When dates written in the month-day-year style occur at the beginning of or in the middle of a sentence, commas should be placed on both sides of the year.

- September 11, 2001, was a sad day for Americans.
- Everyone should return home on Wednesday, October 15, 2012, for the centennial celebration.
- Scott's test date of Thursday, January 14, 2011, has been scheduled for over a year.

Because a comma indicates a short pause, and because people would seldom pause after stating the year in the examples above, Comma Rule #36 seems illogical. Nonetheless, convention dictates using a comma after the year in this situation, and this convention probably will not change any time soon. Therefore, the rule should be followed.

You might occasionally see dates written in what is known as the day-month-year style:

- Hattie was born on 6 July 1933.
- The centennial celebration is scheduled for 15 October 2012.

Chapter 7: Dates, Addresses and City/State Locations, Titles and Designations, Numbers, and Correspondence

Style manuals for a few academic disciplines may require this style, but it should be avoided when possible. Note that commas are *not* used with this date-writing style. Also note that chapter 9 contains two rules about common comma misuses with dates.

## 7.B: Addresses and City/State Locations

### Cities and States

The first comma rule for addresses and locations is applicable whether an address or location is written in a sentence or as a block address for a mailing label.

> Comma Rule #37: A comma should be placed between a city (or a county) and its state.

- Johnny lives in Salem, Massachusetts.
- Have you even been to Kansas City, Missouri?
- George Viking
  104 South Limestone Road
  Rocky, OK 05555

Sometimes a city and state are written at the beginning of or in the middle of a sentence, as in the examples below Comma Rule #38.

> Comma Rule #38: When the city (or county) and state are written at the beginning of or in the middle of a sentence, commas should be placed on both sides of the state.

- Kansas City, Missouri, has a great deal of baseball history.
- Please go to the company's headquarters in Salem, Massachusetts, to claim your prize.

Because a comma indicates a short pause, and because people would seldom pause after naming the state in the examples above,

Chapter 7: Dates, Addresses and City/State Locations, Titles and Designations, Numbers, and Correspondence

Comma Rule #38, like Comma Rule #36, seems illogical. Nonetheless, convention dictates using a comma after the state in this situation, and this convention probably will not change any time soon. Therefore, the rule should be followed.

**Full Addresses**

When writing full addresses in block form, as you would write them for mailing labels or envelopes, line breaks are usually enough to indicate the necessary pauses, and the comma between the city and state is usually the only one that is necessary.

- Jill Nichols
  401 Washington Street
  Tacoma, WA 05555

However, there are two other occasions in which a comma may appear on a single line. Those occasions are addressed in Comma Rule #39 below.

---

Comma Rule #39: Whether an address is written in block form or in a sentence, a comma should separate (1) a street name from a building name and/or a room number and (2) a personal or company name from a title or designation.

---

- *Address that contains both a building name and a room number:*
  Capstone Toys
  9241 Flint Boulevard, Suite 4C
  Firehouse, IN 05555

- *Address that contains both a title and a designation:*
  Cabin Products, Inc.
  Attention: Paul Krauss, Ph.D.
  Pinewood, NY 05555

Chapter 7: Dates, Addresses and City/State Locations, Titles and Designations, Numbers, and Correspondence

(Commas with titles and designations will be addressed in more detail with Comma Rule #41.)

When full addresses are incorporated into a sentence, commas take the place of line breaks.

> Comma Rule #40: When addresses are written in a sentence, commas should be used where line breaks would be used if the address were written in block form, and any commas required within a line in block form should be retained.

- Please mail the package to Jill Nichols, 401 Washington Street, Tacoma, Washington 05555.
- My grandmother's address is 23 North Pike Avenue, Apartment 7, High Mountain, South Dakota 05555.

Note that a comma is never placed between a state and a zip code. Also note that you should spell the names of states when addresses are in a sentence, but abbreviate state names in block addresses.

## 7.C: Titles and Designations

A title may be an abbreviated academic title such as "Ph.D." or a job title such as "Director of Advancement." Designations are usually legal abbreviations that describe a type of company—Inc., Ltd., Llc., etc.

> Comma Rule #41: A comma should precede a title or designation that is used after a personal or company name at the end of a sentence or address line, and commas should be placed on both sides of a title or designation that is used in the middle of a sentence or mailing line.

- John Roberts, M.D.
- Please call Hearty Auto Sales, Inc.
- Diane Stevens, D.D., is the best dentist I know.

- Marty Greenboro, Director of Human Relations, will speak to all employees on Monday.

The reason that titles and designations such as *M.D.*, *Ph.D.*, and *Inc.* require commas is that they are nonrestrictive elements. Recall from chapter 4 that nonrestrictive elements do not affect the meaning of a sentence; they provide "extra" information that could be omitted without consequence. Therefore, Comma Rule #19 from chapter 4 is also applicable to most titles and designations.

Also note that a comma is *not* used when a title appears *before* a name.

- Dr. Rowland went golfing yesterday.
- Professor Bartlett just delivered a great lecture on cloning.
- General Fillmore will retire in 2015.

## 7.D: Numbers

Most people understand how to use commas with numbers, but a couple of rules are worth stating for clarity's sake.

**Regular Numerals**

> Comma Rule #42: Unless a number represents a zip code, a street address, a four-digit year, or a page number, commas should be placed to the left of every third digit in numbers that contain four or more digits.

- 1,298 turtles
- 101,456 towns in cities
- $488,297,444
- 1,333,087,412 trees

Note that this rule represents the only situation in the English language for which writers must work from right to left.

Chapter 7: Dates, Addresses and City/State Locations, Titles and Designations, Numbers, and Correspondence

Omitting the comma in a four-digit number is often acceptable, but you will never be wrong to include it. If you choose to omit the comma in a four-digit number, strive for consistency within a single document. In other words, if you omit the comma in one place, make sure you omit it in all other places as well.

- 1745 pieces of tile   *or*   1,745 pieces of tile

- 1100 boards   *or*   1,100 boards

The exceptions stated in Comma Rule #42 are important. Regardless of how many digits a number contains, never use a comma with a zip code, with a street address, with a page number, or with a four-digit year.

- 05555 (zip code)
- 05555-9999 (zip code)
- 3498 North Walnut Street (street address)
- 23976 Bellhaven Parkway (street address)
- page 1898
- page 10005
- 1994 (year)
- 2014 (year)

Note that a comma *should be* used with a year that contains five or more digits.

- 23,452 BC

**Measurements, Parts, and Categories**

Comma Rule #43: Commas should be used to separate measurements, parts, or categories that communicate a difference in size, space, or scope.

- act III, scene 3
- six feet, seven inches
- chapter 4, part 1
- page 9, line 6
- row 11, seat 23

Measurements, parts, and categories other than those represented in the examples above may exist, and new ones may develop with the evolution of the language.

## 7.E: Correspondence

> Comma Rule #44: Commas should follow salutations (greetings) in informal correspondence and closings in all correspondence.

- Salutations:   Dear Ms. Knight,
  Greetings,
  Professor Kensington,

- Closings:   Sincerely,
  Yours truly,
  Best wishes,
  Respectfully,

While a comma should always follow the salutation in an informal letter, such as a letter to a relative or to an old friend, a colon—instead of a comma—is usually used after a salutation in a business letter, especially if the writer does not know the recipient. The colon communicates a more formal tone for such a situation. However, as Comma Rule #44 states, a comma should *always* follow a *closing* word or phrase.

# Chapter 8
# Difficult Cases and Rules Less Frequently Needed

Chapters 2–7 have addressed the most common comma-related issues and the rules that pertain to them. This chapter addresses a few final rules that do not fit neatly into any certain category. Some of these rules apply to sentence structures that are uncommon. You will seldom need to know some of these rules; in fact, it will be better in many cases to simply revise a sentence so that employing a rule from this chapter is unnecessary. Nonetheless, knowing the rules of this chapter (or being aware of this chapter as a reference) may be helpful.

## 8.A: Serial Items with Internal Commas

From Comma Rule #24 in chapter 5, you have already learned that "Commas should be used to separate all of the items in a series of like elements, and the coordinating conjunction *and* or *or* should be placed after the comma that separates the last and second-to-last items." The sentences below are examples of sentences governed by Comma Rule #24.

- *Linda, Jerry, and Joseph* attended the matinee together. (three words used as subjects)
- *Allie, Jenny, or Lauren* should clean up the mess. (three words used as subjects)
- Joseph *ran, jogged, walked, and stretched* to prepare for the day's game. (four words used as verbs)
- While he was camping, Brett cooked *hamburgers, potatoes, and steaks*. (three words used as direct objects)
- The *red, green, and gold* chair was almost ruined. (three words used as adjectives)

Chapter 8: Difficult Cases and Rules Less Frequently Needed

- Lydia played *by the pool, under the tree, and on the lawn* as she waited for her father. (three adverbial prepositional phrases)
- When Samson's mother returned home, she discovered *that Josie had made a mess on the floor, that Danielle had broken a window, and that Missy had fed the dog too much food.* (three dependent clauses)

Sometimes serial items have commas *within* them, and since using commas both between and within serial items can cause confusion and result in awkward, unclear sentences, there is another rule that applies to such situations. The rule is actually more of a semicolon rule than a comma rule, but it is worth including in this chapter.

Comma Rule #45: When commas are used within serial items, semicolons instead of commas should separate the items themselves.

- Jerry, who is British, plays soccer; Jordan, who is American, plays baseball; and James, who is Canadian, plays polo.
- The candidates were Margaret Whitmore, age 18; Sandy Jansen, age 19; and Molly Flickner, age 19.
- The tour consisted of stops in Kalamazoo, Michigan; Springfield, Missouri; and Chicago.

In the last example above, note that not all of the serial items contain internal commas. (With two of the cities, the state is also mentioned, but the state is not mentioned with *Chicago*.) If more than one item but fewer than all of them contain a comma, semicolons should probably be used, and the item or items that do not require commas should be placed toward the end of the series, provided that placing them there does not alter the meaning of the sentence. If only one item contains an internal comma, as in the example immediately below, commas may be used to separate the items as long as the item without a comma is placed at the end of the series.

- We are going to explore Pennsylvania, Ohio, and Indianapolis, Indiana. (The serial item with internal comma is placed at the end.)

but

- We are going to explore Indianapolis, Indiana; Pennsylvania; and Ohio. (The item with the internal comma is placed at the beginning, so semicolons should be used.)

## 8.B: Placement of Commas When They Are Used with Parentheses

When commas are used with parentheses, the function of the parentheses determines the placement of the comma or commas.

---
Comma Rule #46: When parentheses enclose numbers used to designate serial items in a sentence, an opening parenthesis should be treated as the first word of each serial item.

---

- When you heat the microwave pizza, remember to (1) remove the pizza from the box, (2) remove the plastic wrapping from the pizza, and (3) select the proper cooking time from the microwave's control panel.
- Margaret told her oldest son to (1) take out the trash, (2) wash the dishes, (3) clean his room, and (4) change the oil in the car.

Note that the final comma is placed between the second-to-last serial item and the word *and*, not between the word *and* and the final opening parenthesis for the final number. In other words, the final opening parenthesis is treated as the first word of the final serial item would normally be treated.

The other occasion for which you may need to use a comma with parentheses is when you use parenthetical information in the middle of sentence (see chapter 4, Comma Rule #20).

Chapter 8: Difficult Cases and Rules Less Frequently Needed

> Comma Rule #47: When text within parentheses interrupts the usual placement of a comma, the comma should be placed immediately after the closing parenthesis.

- Nadia's painting was beautiful (she worked on it for months), and her sculpture wasn't bad, either. (The comma is needed to separate the two independent clauses that are joined by the coordinating conjunction *and*.)
- Along the riverbank (which is teeming with insects), George is teaching his two youngest children how to fish. (The comma is needed to follow the introductory prepositional phrase.)
- Enjoying the show (the comedian on television was quite funny), Joel forgot about the food that was in the oven. (The comma is needed to follow the introductory participial phrase.)

## 8.C: "The More," "The Better," "The Greater," and Similar Phrases

Although sentence constructions based on "The more...the greater..." contrasts are rare, knowing how and when to use commas with them can only improve your writing.

> Comma Rule #48: Use a comma to separate "the more...the greater..." type sentence elements unless the elements are very short.

The difference between "long" and "short" as presented in Comma Rule #48 is somewhat subjective. Generally, a comma should separate the elements if they are longer than three or four words.

- The more you study for your test, the better your grade will be in the class.
- The fewer people who care about participating in the democratic process, the more the government will decide things for us.

Chapter 8: Difficult Cases and Rules Less Frequently Needed

- The bigger they are, the harder they fall.
but
- The bigger the better.

(Note that such constructions are grammatical anomalies; they are not really complete sentences because neither clause is independent.)

# 8.D: Internal Monologue

**Internal Monologue That Follows Explanatory Information and Ends a Sentence**

In chapter 6, you learned how to use commas with quotations and dialogue. Depending on the placement of a quotation or speech within a sentence, a comma may be placed either inside or outside of quotation marks.

- Mandy screamed to her little brother, "Get out of my room!"
- "I was looking for my skateboard," her brother replied.

**Internal monologue** is the term used for words that characters think to themselves. Internal monologue is usually introduced or followed by words and phrases such as *thought [to himself]*, *wondered [to herself]*, *pondered*, *asked [herself]* and so forth. Just as the word *said* has many substitutes, the word *thought* has substitutes that serve to signal internal monologue.

- *I wish had brought more money with me,* Dillon thought to himself when he saw the stereo on the store shelf.
- Pamela wondered as she tried on her new shoes, *Do I really care what everyone else thinks of what I am wearing?*
- Lisa asked herself as she sat across the table from her date, *Does he think I am interested in him?*

In the examples above, note that the internal monologue is italicized. While not all professional writers use italics for internal monologue, many do, and it is a good practice to do so. The use of italics distinguishes internal monologue from dialogue and quotations, which are placed in quotation marks.

Chapter 6 rules that govern comma usage with quotations are similar to the rules that govern comma usage with internal monologue. Those rules are slightly revised below, and each rule contains examples below it.

> Comma Rule #49: When internal monologue that ends a sentence follows explanatory information containing the word *thought* or one of its substitutes, and when the internal monologue does not blend with the grammatical structure of the sentence, a comma should be placed immediately after the explanatory information that precedes the quotation.

Probably the most common way to use internal monologue in a sentence is to use explanatory information and the word *thought* or one of its substitutes *before* the monologue. Like the first word in a quotation, the first word in an internal monologue should be capitalized.

- John thought to himself, *I wish she would leave me alone.*
- After he ate dinner, Uncle Joe relaxed in his chair and thought to himself, *I wonder if Aunt Irene knows how bad that ham is.*
- Staring at a large audience, the guest speaker wondered, *Will they love me or hate me?*

Notice that the internal monologues in the examples above do not blend with the grammatical structure of the sentences in which they are contained. Rather, they are grammatical structures all their own; that is, they could stand alone as complete thoughts.

When internal monologue *does* blend with the grammatical structure of the sentence, a comma should *not* precede it. Often, internal monologue can be blended with the grammatical structure of a sentence by simply placing a word such as *that* or *if* before it.

Chapter 8: Difficult Cases and Rules Less Frequently Needed

- The doctor thought *that* Shelby had lost too much weight.
- Lori wondered *if* the storm would destroy the house.

In both of the examples above, a comma would be used after the introductory verb if the word *that* or *if* were omitted.

- The doctor thought to himself, *Shelby has lost too much weight.*
- Lori wondered, *Will the storm destroy the house?*

Adding *that* or *if* enables the internal monologue to blend with the grammatical structure of the sentences. In fact, when blended with the grammatical structure of a sentence as in the first two examples above, note that internal monologue is not really internal monologue at all. It is not italicized, and it simply completes a normal sentence.

## Internal Monologue That Begins a Sentence and Is Followed by Explanatory Information

Internal monologue may also appear at the beginning of a sentence—*before* the explanatory information. A rule similar to Comma Rule #49 guides comma usage for such instances.

> Comma Rule #50: When internal monologue begins a sentence and is followed by explanatory information containing the word *thought* or one of its substitutes, a comma should be placed immediately after the internal monologue.

- *We need a bigger house,* Suzie thought as she put away her clothes.
- *Please send us some rain,* George prayed silently.

When a question mark or an exclamation point is used at the end of an internal monologue that begins a sentence, no comma is used between the monologue and the explanatory information that follows.

- *I am so mad!* the boy thought after his mother grounded him.

- *Are we there yet?* the little girl wondered.
- *Who made this mess?* Collin asked himself as he walked into his kitchen.

Note from the examples above that the first word of the explanatory information is not capitalized unless it is a proper noun or adjective.

## Internal Monologue That Occurs in the Middle of a Sentence

Sometimes internal monologues have explanatory information both before and after them.

> Comma Rule #51: When internal monologue occurs in the middle of a sentence and is either preceded by or followed by explanatory information containing the word *thought* or one of its substitutes, and when the internal monologue does not blend with the grammatical structure of the sentence, a comma should be placed immediately after the explanatory information to its left and immediately after the end of the monologue, unless the end of the monologue requires a question mark or an exclamation point.

- Ian thought, *Those clouds are moving toward us*, but he did not seek shelter.
- After the game, the coach thought to himself, *I am very proud of my players*, but he did not share the thought with the team.

In each of the examples above, the words that follow the internal monologue begin with a coordinating conjunction (*but*). This arrangement will most often be the case when an internal monologue occurs in the middle of a sentence.

When a question mark or an exclamation point is used at the end of an internal monologue that occurs in the middle of a sentence, no comma is needed.

Chapter 8: Difficult Cases and Rules Less Frequently Needed

- The young child thought to himself, *What a game!* and then he unknowingly began to dance.
- The rancher asked himself, *What more can I do to keep my livestock out of my neighbor's field?* for he had exhausted every known possibility.
- When traveling, the little girl often wonders to herself, *Are we there yet?* but she does not voice the question to her father because she knows it is a question that annoys him.

## Internal Monologue That Is Divided by Explanatory Information

> Comma Rule #52: When internal monologue is divided by explanatory information, a comma should be placed immediately after the first part of the monologue, immediately before the second part, and immediately after the second part if the second part does not end the sentence.

The sentences immediately below serve as examples of how to use commas with internal monologues that are divided by explanatory information.

- *This restaurant's salsa,* thought the customer, *is the best in the city.*
- *When summer arrives,* Melissa mentally noted, *the beach will be my home.*
- *I'm tired,* thought Tina, *but I don't want to go home yet.*

In the examples above, note that the first word in the second part of the monologue (*is*, *the*, and *but*) is *not* capitalized because the second part of the monologue is simply a continuation of the first part. Also note that the second part of the monologue ends the sentence, so the punctuation that ends the monologue also serves as the punctuation that ends the entire sentence. When non-monologue information appears after the second part of the monologue, a comma should be placed after the second part of the monologue.

- *This restaurant's salsa,* thought the customer, is *the best in the city,* so he decided to return next week.
- *I'm tired,* thought Tina, *and I want to go home,* but she still had much work to do.

## 8.E: Questions Referred to Within Sentences

Occasionally in a sentence, you may wish to *refer* to a question, not necessarily ask one.

Comma Rule #53: A question referenced within a sentence should be preceded by a comma.

- The question, where did I place my keys? is one that I ask often.
- Everyone wanted to know the answer to the question, how did the magician do that?

Note from the examples above that a comma does *not* follow a question, even if it appears in the middle of a sentence, for the question is already punctuated with a question mark. Also note that the first word of a question referenced within a sentence does *not* need to be capitalized.

These types of sentence constructions can be awkward, and they usually can be avoided by simply changing the sentence structure.

- The question, where did I place my keys? is one that I ask often.
  or
- I often ask myself where I have placed my keys.
- Everyone wanted to know the answer to the question, how did the magician do that?
  or
- Everyone wanted to know how the magician did that.

Chapter 8: Difficult Cases and Rules Less Frequently Needed

While sentences containing questions that are referenced as questions may usually be avoided, there may be times, nonetheless, when you absolutely have to reference a question within a sentence, so you can benefit from knowing how to use commas at such times.

# 8.F: "Not Only...But Also..." Sentence Constructions

Comma usage with "not only...but also..." sentence constructions is determined by the function of the "not only...but also..." elements.

> Comma Rule #54: When each element of a "not only...but also..." sentence construction contains both a subject and a verb, a comma should separate the clauses.

The sentences below serve as examples for Comma Rule #54. In each clause, the subject is underlined once and the verb is underlined twice. Note that the word *but* is sometimes merely implied (as in the second sentence below) when both parts of the construction contain both a subject and a verb.

- Pam not only grows prize tomatoes, but she also wins blue ribbons for her pumpkins.
- My uncle not only fought bravely in the World War II, he also stopped a bank robbery one time in Tampa, Florida.

When "not only...but also..." elements do *not* contain both a subject and a verb, the rule for comma usage is not as rigid.

> Comma Rule #55: When the elements of a "not only...but also..." sentence construction do not contain both a subject and a verb, a comma should not be used to separate the elements unless the text between "not only" and "but also" phrases is long and the meeting place of the two phrases would necessitate a natural pause if the sentence were read aloud.

- Jason played the game not only with skill but also with poise. (In this sentence, *not only* and *but also* introduce prepositional phrases. The elements lack a subject and verb.)
- Juliet taught her children not only to be wise but also to be nice. (In this sentence, *not only* and *but also* introduce infinitive phrases, not clauses.)
- Parker bought not only shoes but also shirts. (In this sentence, *not only* and *but also* simply separate two nouns that serve as direct objects—*shoes* and *shirts*.)

No commas are needed in the examples above. If, however, there is so much text between the "not only" and "but also" elements that a short pause would make the sentence easier to read, you may use a comma to separate the elements, even if they do not contain both a subject and a verb.

- Juliet taught her children to be wise not only in choosing their friends and social activities, but also in interacting with people both at work and at play. (*Not only* and *but also* introduce prepositional phrases. Neither element contains both a subject and a verb, but the comma after *activities* may help make the sentence easier to read since a reader would likely pause for a short breath after the word *activities*.)

# 8.G: Homonyms That Appear Beside Each Other

**Homonyms** are words that are spelled and pronounced the same but have different functions. When homonyms appear beside each other in a sentence, readers usually do a double-take at the text, thinking that a word has probably been unnecessarily typed twice. Thus, homonyms that appear beside each other result in an awkward situation.

- *Awkward*: He walked in in blue jeans.

# Chapter 8: Difficult Cases and Rules Less Frequently Needed

> Comma Rule #56: To facilitate understanding and easier reading, a comma may separate homonyms that appear beside each other in a sentence, except in sentences involving "that/that" constructions.

- He walked in, in blue jeans.
- The one plant that grew, grew large.

Notice that Comma Rule #56 states that a comma *may* separate homonyms that appear beside each other in a sentence. It is impossible to declare that a comma should be used in every such situation. If a slight pause would occur between the homonyms when read aloud, then a comma is most likely appropriate. If a pause would not occur, a writer should use his or her best judgment when faced with such sentence constructions. Even with commas, however, such constructions are awkward, so they should be avoided if possible.

The exception to Comma Rule #56 involves sentences with "that/that" constructions.

- Ann said that that dog was causing trouble at the party.
- Don't you know that that shirt is too small?

## 8.H: Commas to Indicate Omission

When writing serial items, writers sometimes omit words that would ordinarily be expressed in a non-serial context. Consider the following sentences, for example:

- *Non-serial context*: Shelly went to New Jersey for the summer.
- *Serial context*: For the summer, Shelly went to New Jersey; Joe, Maine; and Robin, North Carolina.

In the second sentence above, the words *went to* have been omitted from the last two serial items. However, readers still understand the sentence.

## Chapter 8: Difficult Cases and Rules Less Frequently Needed

> Comma Rule #57: Commas may be used in the place of words omitted from serial items.

- For Christmas I hope we go to Grandpa Smith's house; for Thanksgiving, Aunt Josie's; and for Memorial Day, Uncle Phil's.
- The Tigers defeated the Red Sox 5–4; the Rangers, 7–2; and the Yankees, 9–0.

Often, as with other sentence constructions addressed in this chapter, the type of sentence construction described in this section can be avoided.

- I hope we go to Grandpa Smith's house for Christmas, to Aunt Josie's for Thanksgiving, and to Uncle Phil's for Memorial Day.

Nevertheless, knowing Comma Rule #57 can be helpful occasionally.

Note that Comma Rule #57 states that commas *may* be used in the place of words omitted from serial items. In some sentences, commas might not be necessary. For example, they may be omitted when only one or two—not all—of the words that would ordinarily be used have been omitted.

- The first contestant's strength was singing, the second's was dancing, and the third's was playing the guitar.

In the sentence above, the word *contestant's* is omitted from the second and third items in the series. Since *contestant's* is the only word omitted, the serial items do not need internal commas. If, however, the word *was* were also omitted, the sentence would benefit from the application of Comma Rule #57.

- The first contestant's strength was singing; the second's, dancing; and the third's, playing the guitar.

Chapter 8: Difficult Cases and Rules Less Frequently Needed

# 8.I: Sentences Containing Two Introductory Elements

Recall from chapter 3 that an **introductory element** is a grammatical unit that precedes the traditional subject (including any subject descriptors) + verb sentence construction. Occasionally, a sentence may have two introductory elements. Consider the sentences below.

    Transitional      Dependent Clause
    Expression

- <u>Of course,</u> <u>if Hannah leaves a day early</u> she will also be able to stop at the museum in Philadelphia.

    Transitional  Prepositional
    Expression     phrase

- <u>However,</u> <u>in the winter</u> the drive will be more difficult.

    Interjection   Pair of Prepositional Phrases

- <u>Yes,</u> <u>in the laundry basket</u> <u>by the door</u> you will find your new shirt.

Sentences such as the ones above leave writers with difficult choices, for none of the rules presented in this book neatly addresses every situation in which more than one introductory element may begin a sentence. However, Comma Rule #58, which offers guidance but also encourages discretion and choice on the part of the writer, may be helpful.

Chapter 8: Difficult Cases and Rules Less Frequently Needed

> Comma Rule #58: When two introductory elements begin a sentence, a comma should be placed after the first element, but the pause principle and authorial preference should govern the use of a comma after the second element, unless the second element is a transitional expression or a very long element that would naturally necessitate a breathing pause if the sentence were spoken—then a comma should be used.

In each of the three example sentences above, a comma is placed after the first introductory element but not after the second. Technically, placing a comma after each of the second introductory elements would not be wrong; however, a pause after the second introductory element of each sentence would be, arguably, unnatural. In the sentences below, on the other hand, note that commas are placed after both the first and the second introductory elements.

- Matthew does not sleep well when just the fan is going. <u>When the air conditioner is on</u>, <u>however</u>, he sleeps like a baby.

In the sentence above, the first underlined unit is a dependent clause, and the second underlined unit is the conjunctive adverb/transitional expression *however*. In situations such as the one represented by this sentence, note that Comma Rule #58 actually restates Comma Rule #21 from chapter 4: "Commas should be placed around a conjunctive adverb or other transitional expression that occurs in the middle of a sentence and *precedes* the main verb…" In other words, in the sentence above, the first comma does double duty: it follows the introductory element, but it also sets off to the left the transitional expression *however*.

Now consider another sentence.

- <u>Yes</u>, <u>when the ice cream truck makes it way from the elementary school to the neighbor's house across the street</u>, you may buy a chocolate sundae.

In this sentence, a comma follows *both* introductory elements—the opening interjection *yes* as well as the dependent clause that follows it.

## Chapter 8: Difficult Cases and Rules Less Frequently Needed

A comma is used after the second introductory element because it is relatively long and would more than likely necessitate a breathing pause if it were spoken aloud. For the sake of comparison, though, consider again a sentence that contains a *shorter* second element.

- <u>Yes,</u> <u>when the ice cream truck arrives</u> you may buy a chocolate sundae.

In the sentence immediately above, the second introductory element, the dependent clause, has been shortened. A writer may or may not include a comma after the dependent clause in this sentence because the dependent clause might not necessitate a breathing pause if it were spoken aloud.

Finally, it is important to remember that certain introductory elements, when combined, may actually function as one element. For instance, recall from chapter 3 that a dependent clause that follows a sentence-beginning prepositional phrase may simply "complete" the prepositional phrase in order to comprise a single descriptive unit.

- *Under an umbrella* **because the <u>rain</u> <u>was falling</u> hard**, Joey ran quickly to his car.
- *On fire* **until the <u>rain</u> <u>fell</u>,** the field's crops were destroyed.

Similarly, recall from chapter 3 that a prepositional phrase or a dependent clause—or a combination of both—usually "completes" a participial phrase and is therefore considered part of the participial phrase.

- *Questioned <u>about his involvement</u> <u>in the crime</u> **because he was so close to the scene**,* the man began to regret what he had done.
- *Helping **in various ways whenever she sees an opportunity**,* the woman is proving to be a wonderful asset to the firm.
- *Carrying on <u>about his days</u> <u>as an athlete</u> **as if people are interested in his stories**,* Richard is driving people away from the party.

# Chapter 9
# Common Comma Misuses

Arguably, using a comma where a comma does not belong can affect one's writing even more negatively than not using a comma in places where one should be used. Many of the rules presented in this chapter have been stated throughout the book by association with other rules. However, this chapter will provide more detail about some of those issues.

## 9.A: The Comma Splice

The comma splice is perhaps the most common comma-related mistake. It is actually more about incompleteness than total incorrectness, however.

Recall Comma Rule #1 from chapter 2: "A sentence comprised of two independent clauses or complete thoughts should be joined by both a comma and a coordinating conjunction, and the comma should be placed immediately after the first clause or complete thought." The term *coordinating conjunction* is the key element of this rule. When a writer forgets to use a coordinating conjunction and instead uses *only* a comma to join two independent clauses, the writer has committed the error of the comma splice. (Remember that there are only seven coordinating conjunctions in the English language: *for, and, nor, but, or, yet, so*.)

- *Incorrect*: Sophia took a walk in the park, Mr. Garcia took his children with him to the supermarket.

The sentence above is an example of a comma splice. The comma incorrectly *splices* two independent clauses.

## Chapter 9: Common Comma Misuses

> Comma Rule #59: Do not use *only* a comma to join two independent clauses or complete thoughts—a coordinating conjunction must accompany the comma.

- *Incorrect*: Sophia took a walk in the park, Mr. Garcia took his children with him to the supermarket.
- *Correct*: Sophia took a walk in the park, and Mr. Garcia took his children with him to the supermarket.

- *Incorrect*: Jerry watched television all night, Robert went to bed early.
- *Correct:* Jerry watched television all night, and Robert went to bed early.

- *Incorrect*: Teachers should be paid more money, they are invaluable to society.
- *Correct*: Teachers should be paid more money, for they are invaluable to society.

- *Incorrect*: The bank in his hometown would not accept his check, Lou was forced to drive ten miles to the nearest ATM machine.
- *Correct*: The bank in his hometown would not accept his check, so Lou was forced to drive ten miles to the nearest ATM machine.

Be aware that some comma splices can also be corrected by simply creating two sentences or by joining the two independent clauses with a semicolon. The approach a writer chooses depends on his or her intent and the context. A semicolon can be used only if the two clauses are closely related. All of the statements below are punctuated correctly.

- Sophia took a walk in the park. Mr. Garcia took his children with him to the supermarket.

- Sophia took a walk in the park; Mr. Garcia took his children with him to the supermarket.
- Sophia took a walk in the park, [and/but] Mr. Garcia took his children with him to the supermarket.

## 9.B: Compound Elements

As stated in chapter 5, a *series*, in grammatical terms, is defined as a group of *three or more* like elements that appear within a sentence and are used together. Serial items must be separated by commas, and the word *and* (or occasionally the word *or*) should appear between the last two items.

- *Linda, Jerry, and Joseph* attended the matinee together. (three words used as subjects)
- *Allie, Jenny, or Lauren* should clean up the mess. (three words used as subjects)
- Joseph *ran, jogged, walked, and stretched* to prepare for the day's game. (four words used as verbs)
- While he was camping, Brett cooked *hamburgers, potatoes, and steaks*. (three words used as direct objects)
- The *red, green, and gold* chair was almost ruined. (three words used as adjectives)
- Lydia played *by the pool, under the tree, and on the lawn* as she waited for her father. (three adverbial prepositional phrases)
- When Samson's mother returned home, she discovered *that Josie had made a mess on the floor, that Danielle had broken a window, and that Missy had fed the dog too much food*. (three dependent clauses)

Writers must understand that only *two* like elements do not constitute a series.

Comma Rule #60: Do not use a comma between only two like elements unless a comma is necessitated by another rule.

## Chapter 9: Common Comma Misuses

Most people understand Comma Rule #60 as it applies to words or phrases.

- *Incorrect*: Linda, and Jerry attended the matinee together. (two words used as subjects)
- *Correct*: Linda and Jerry attended the matinee together.

- *Incorrect*: Joseph *ran*, and *stretched* to prepare for the day's game. (two words used as verbs)
- *Correct*: Joseph *ran* and *stretched* to prepare for the day's game.

- *Incorrect*: While he was camping, Brett cooked *hamburgers*, and *steaks*. (two words used as direct objects)
- *Correct*: While he was camping, Brett cooked *hamburgers* and *steaks*.

- *Incorrect*: The *red*, and *yellow* chair was almost ruined. (two words used as adjectives)
- *Correct*: The *red* and *yellow* chair was almost ruined.

- *Incorrect*: Linda played *by the pool*, and *on the lawn* as she waited for her father. (two adverbial prepositional phrases)
- *Correct*: Linda played *by the pool* and *on the lawn* as she waited for her father.

The majority of mistakes related to this issue revolve around misusing a comma with two *verb phrases*. Mistakes such as the one in the sentence below are common.

- *Incorrect*: In an effort to gain national recognition, <u>the college added a number of new academic majors</u>, and <u>expanded its budget for its honors program</u>.

The second comma in the sentence above should not be there. In making such errors, writers make one of two possible mistakes. They either incorrectly define *series* as only two items, or they consider the compound verb phrases (double underlined) to be two independent

## Chapter 9: Common Comma Misuses

clauses. The sentence above does not contain two independent clauses, however. Instead, the subject *college* simply has two verbs—*added* and *expanded*. The sentence may be correctly revised in two ways.

- *Correct*: In an effort to gain national recognition, the college added a number of new academic majors and expanded its budget for its honors program. (No comma is needed after *majors* because the sentence simply contains two verb phrases—*added a number of new academic majors* and *expanded its budget for its honors program*—for the same subject, *college*.)
- *Correct*: In an effort to gain national recognition, the college added a number of new academic majors, and **it** expanded its budget for its honors program. (In this sentence, the word *it* has been added. Now, since *it* functions as the subject of an independent clause, the coordinating conjunction *and* separates two independent clauses. Comma Rule #1 from chapter 2 is therefore applicable: "A sentence comprised of two independent clauses or complete thoughts should be joined by both a comma and a coordinating conjunction, and the comma should be placed immediately after the first clause or complete thought." Without the word *it*, the sentence simply contains two verb phrases that have the same subject: *college*.)

Be aware, however, that some other comma rule may necessitate a comma between two items.

- Joe, who played the trumpet, and Patrick, who played the trombone, were excellent in Tuesday night's performance. (*Who played the trumpet* and *who played the trombone* are nonrestrictive clauses [see Comma Rule #19 from chapter 4], so commas are used between the compound subjects *Joe* and *Patrick*.)

## 9.C: Comma Misuse with Subordinating Conjunctions

Another misuse of the comma involves its placement after a subordinating conjunction. (If necessary, review the list of common subordinating conjunctions from table 2.2 in chapter 2.)

> Comma Rule #61: Do not use a comma immediately after a subordinating conjunction unless a comma is necessitated by another rule.

- *Incorrect*: Although, I cleaned my room on Saturday morning, I forgot to make my bed.
- *Correct*: Although I cleaned my room on Saturday evening, I forgot to make my bed.

- *Incorrect*: You should go finish your homework unless, you want to be in trouble.
- *Correct*: You should go finish your homework unless you want to be in trouble.

In the sentences above, *although* and *unless* are subordinating conjunctions that begin dependent clauses.

Below is an example of a comma that is placed after a subordinating conjunction because of another rule.

- Jerry won the contest *because*, after all, he was the best. (The phrase *after all* is a minimally interruptive parenthetical expression, so Comma Rule #20 from Chapter 4 is applied.)

## 9.D: Dates, Holidays, and Seasons

Comma Rules #35 and #36 from chapter 7 address comma usage with dates. Below are two rules pertaining to common comma misuses with dates.

Chapter 9: Common Comma Misuses

> Comma Rule #62: Do not use a comma when writing only the month and day or month and year.

- *Incorrect*: She lost her purse on July, 20.
- *Correct*: She lost her purse on July 20.

- *Incorrect*: He dropped his wallet in the lake in September, 2003.
- *Correct*: He dropped his wallet in the lake in September 2003.

The next rule pertaining to comma misuse with dates is similar to Comma Rule #62 above.

> Comma Rule #63: Do not use a comma between a season and a year or between the name of a specific holiday and year.

- *Incorrect*: Summer, 1993 was an unforgettable time.
- *Correct*: Summer 1993 was an unforgettable time.

- *Incorrect*: My dad tricked me on Halloween, 1999.
- *Correct*: My dad tricked me on Halloween 1999.

## 9.E: Family Titles

Comma Rule #41 from chapter 7 states, "A comma should precede a title or designation that is used after a personal or company name at the end of a sentence or address line, and commas should be placed on both sides of a title or designation that is used in the middle of a sentence or mailing line." A few examples of Comma Rule #41 properly demonstrated are below.

- John Roberts, M.D.
- Please call Hearty Auto Sales, Inc.
- Diane Stevens, D.D., is the best dentist I know.
- Marty Greenboro, Director of Human Relations, will speak to all employees on Monday.

The reason that titles and designations such as *M.D., Ph.D.,* and *Inc.* require commas is that they are nonrestrictive elements. Recall from chapter 4 that nonrestrictive elements do not affect the meaning of a sentence; they provide "extra" information that could be omitted without consequence. Therefore, Comma Rule #19 from chapter 4 is also applicable to most titles and designations.

However, note that family titles such as *Jr., Sr., II,* and *III* are restrictive. For instance, Larry Rose Jr. is a different person than Larry Rose. The family title *Jr.* is restrictive; therefore, writers should observe Comma Rule #64 when using family titles.

> Comma Rule #64: Do not use a comma with restrictive family titles such as *Jr., Sr., II, III,* etc.

- *Incorrect*: The package should be addressed to Michael Willowby, III.
- *Correct*: The package should be addressed to Michael Willowby III.

- *Incorrect*: Victor Barron, Jr., is a film director in California.
- *Correct*: Victor Barron Jr. is a film director in California.

# 9.F: Elements Not Usually Separated by Commas

### Subjects and Their Verbs

> Comma Rule #65: Do not use a comma between a subject and its verb(s) unless a comma is necessitated by another rule.

- *Incorrect*: The secretary's <u>report,</u> <u>indicated</u> that too much money was spent on party supplies last year. (The comma is unnecessary in this sentence.)
- *Correct*: The secretary's <u>report</u> <u>indicated</u> that too much money was spent on party supplies last year.

- *Correct*: The secretary's <u>report</u>, which was released yesterday, <u>indicated</u> that too much money was spent on party supplies last year. (In this sentence, *which was released yesterday* is a non-restrictive clause, so the commas between the subject *report* and its verb *indicated* are appropriate. See Comma Rule #19 from chapter 4.)

## Action Verbs and Their Complements

Many sentences written in English contain **objects**. Recall from chapter 1 that **direct objects** are the words that receive the action of an action verb. They are italicized in the sentences below.

- Caleb made *pies* with his mother. (*Pies* are what Caleb *made*.)
- The company recalled its newest *car* because a faulty part was a fire hazard. (The *car* is what the company *recalled*.)
- The thief stole the couple's new *television*. (The *television* is what the thief *stole*.)

Recall from chapter 1 that **indirect objects** are nouns or pronouns that identify to whom or what or for whom or what a verb's action is performed. They usually precede direct objects. Indirect objects are underlined once in the sentences below, and direct objects are underlined twice.

- Caleb gave his <u>mother</u> some <u>pies</u>.
- The company told its <u>customers</u> a few <u>lies</u>.
- The thief owes the <u>Smiths</u> a new <u>television</u>.

> Comma Rule #66: Do not use a comma between an action verb and its object(s) unless a comma is necessitated by another rule.

- *Incorrect*: The thief stole, the couple's new television. (The comma is unnecessary in this sentence.)
- *Correct*: The thief stole the couple's new television.

- *Correct*: The thief stole, rather clumsily, the couple's new television. (In this sentence, *rather clumsily* is a nonrestrictive phrase, so the commas between the verb *stole* and the object *television* is appropriate. See Comma Rule #19 from chapter 4.)

## Linking Verbs and Their Complements

Note that the verbs in the section above are action verbs. Some sentences contain *linking verbs*. Recall from chapter 1 that linking verbs are verbs such as *is, are, be, were, was,* etc. Some verbs can be either linking verbs or action verbs: *feel, smell, look, seem, appear,* etc. Linking verbs have what are called *predicate complements*, which may be categorized as either *predicate nominatives* or *predicate adjectives*. If the complement *identifies* or *renames* the subject, then it is a predicate nominative.

- The speaker is an *expert* in American history.
- The building is a *fortress*.

If the complement *describes* the subject, then it is a predicate adjective.

- The speaker is *silly*.
- The building is *old*.

When speaking, we usually do not pause between a linking verb and a predicate complement, so a comma normally is not used between these two elements in writing.

---
Comma Rule #67: Do not use a comma between a linking verb and its predicate complement(s) unless a comma is necessitated by another rule.

---

- *Incorrect*: The speaker is, silly. (The comma is unnecessary in this sentence.)
- *Correct*: The speaker is silly.

- *Correct*: The speaker is, according to many, quite silly. (In this sentence, the phrase *according to many* is a minimally interruptive parenthetical phrase, so the commas between the linking verb *is* and the subject complement *silly* are appropriate. See Comma Rule #20 from chapter 4.)

## Prepositions and Their Objects

Recall that prepositional phrases begin with a preposition and end with a noun or pronoun, which is called the *object* of the preposition. Some prepositional phrases also contain adjectives that describe the objects. (If necessary, review the list of the most common prepositions in chapter 3, Table 3.2)

- *on the beach* (**on** [preposition] **the** [modifies *beach*] **beach** [noun/object of phrase])
- *in summer* (**in** [preposition] **summer** [noun/object of phrase])
- *above the blue sky* (**above** [preposition] **the** [modifies *sky*] **blue** [modifies *sky*] **sky** [noun/object of phrase])
- *with elegance* (**with** [preposition] **elegance** [noun/object of preposition])
- *in his deceitful way* (**in** [preposition] **his** [modifies *way*] **deceitful** [modifies *way*] **way** [noun/object of phrase])

When speaking, we usually do not pause between a preposition and its object or objects, so a comma is not normally used between these two elements in writing.

Comma Rule #68: Do not use a comma between a preposition and its object(s) unless a comma is necessitated by another rule.

- *Incorrect*: After we arrived at the beach house, we took a nice walk along, the shore. (The second comma is unnecessary.)
- *Correct*: After we arrived at the beach house, we took a nice long walk along the shore.

- *Correct*: After we arrived at the beach house, we took a nice walk along the crowded, but not overcrowded, shoreline. (In this sentence, the phrase *but not overcrowded* is a contrasting element, so the commas are appropriate even though they are placed between the preposition *along* and its object, *shoreline*. See Comma Rule #23 from chapter 4.)

**Prepositional Phrases That Follow Other Major Sentence Elements**

When speaking, we usually do not pause between a major sentence element such as subject, verb, or complement and a prepositional phrase that follows it, so a comma is not normally used before a prepositional phrase.

---
Comma Rule #69: Do not use a comma between a major sentence element such as a subject, verb, or complement and a prepositional phrase unless a comma is necessitated by another rule.

---

- *Incorrect*: Cowboys, on horses are seen often in Pasture County, Montana. (The subject *cowboys* is followed immediately by the prepositional phrase *on horses*. The comma between these two elements should not be there.)
- *Correct*: Cowboys on horses are often seen in Pasture County, Montana.

- *Incorrect*: The cowboys rode, on horses for many hours. (The verb *rode* is followed immediately by the prepositional phrase *on horses*. The comma between these two elements should not be there.)
- *Correct*: The cowboys rode on horses for many hours.

- *Incorrect*: Riding, on horses, the cowboys set out to find the lost calf. (The participle *riding* is followed immediately by the prepositional phrase *on horses*. The comma between these two elements should not be there, for the prepositional phrase simply completes the participial phrase that begins with participle *riding*. The second comma is needed because *Riding on horses* is a participial phrase that begins a sentence. See Comma Rule #16 from chapter 3.)

- *Correct*: Riding on horses, the cowboys set out to find the lost calf.

- *Incorrect*: Cody placed the shoes, on the horse's hooves before he rode away. (The direct object *shoes* is followed immediately by the prepositional phrase *on the horse's hooves*. The comma between these two elements should not be there.)
- *Correct*: Cody placed the shoes on the horse's hooves before he rode away.

Only when necessitated by another rule should a comma be used between a major sentence element and a prepositional phrase that follows it. The sentences below contain examples of such exceptions.

- The cowboys, in their own version of heaven under the massive starry sky, decided to sing songs around the campfire. (In this sentence, the prepositional phrases *in their own version*, *of heaven*, and *under the massive starry sky* collectively comprise a nonrestrictive element, so the comma between them and the subject *cowboys* is appropriate. See Comma Rule #19 from chapter 4.)
- The cowboys rode, against the wishes of their wives, for almost forty miles in blistering heat. (In this sentence, the prepositional phrases *against the wishes* and *of their wives* are nonrestrictive phrases, so the comma between them and the verb *rode* is appropriate. See Comma Rule #19 from chapter 4.)
- Walking, not riding, through the pastureland, the cowboys were determined to find the lost calf. (In this sentence, *not riding* is a contrasting element, so the commas between the present participle *walking* and the prepositional phrase *through the pastureland* are appropriate. See Comma Rule #23 from chapter 4.)
- Cody placed the saddle, which was quite worn, on the horse's back. (In this sentence, the dependent clause *which was quite*

Chapter 9: Common Comma Misuses

*worn* is a nonrestrictive clause, so the commas between the direct object *saddle* and the prepositional phrase *on the horse's back* are appropriate. See Comma Rule #19 from chapter 4.)

## 9.G: First and Last Items in a Series

Recall from chapter 5 that a *series* is defined as three or more like elements that appear together within a sentence. As stated in Comma Rule #24, "Commas should be used to separate all of the items in a series of like elements, and the coordinating conjunction *and* or *or* should be placed after the comma that separates the last and second-to-last items."

- The girl ran, jumped, and bounced on the trampoline. (three words)
- The boy played baseball, cleaned his room, and ate his dinner. (three phrases)
- Ashley went to Minneapolis, Kendra went to Chicago, and Jessica went to Green Bay. (three independent clauses)

Chapter 5 addresses the placement of commas with serial items, but the rule of where *not* to place commas with serial items is worth emphasizing here.

> Comma Rule #70: Do not use a comma before the first item or after the last item in a series unless a comma is necessitated by another rule.

- *Incorrect*: I spend most of my spare time, *reading, writing,* and *studying*. (The first comma should not be there. No other rule necessitates a comma before the first item in the series.)
- *Correct*: I spend most of my spare time *reading, writing, and studying*.

- *Correct*: I spend most of my spare time, which I don't have much of these days, *reading, writing, and studying*. (In this sentence, *which I don't have much of these days* is a nonrestrictive

128

Chapter 9: Common Comma Misuses

clause, so the comma before the first serial item—*reading*—is appropriate. See Comma Rule #19 from chapter 4.)

- *Incorrect*: I spend most of my spare time *reading, writing,* and *studying,* in the library. (The comma after *studying* should not be there. No other rule necessitates a comma after the last item in the series.)
- *Correct*: I spend most of my spare time *reading, writing, and studying,* so I don't watch much television. (In this sentence, the comma after the final serial item separates two independent clauses that are joined by a coordinating conjunction, so the comma is appropriate. See Comma Rule #1 from chapter 2.)

## 9.H: First and Last Coordinate Adjectives

As explained in chapter 5, coordinate adjectives are adjectives that appear beside each other and "equally" describe the same noun(s) or pronoun(s).

- Johnson tried to avoid the *smoky, dingy* bar.
- The *rickety, dangerous* elevator frightened all who looked upon it.
- *Windy, slick* roads should be avoided, especially at night.

As the examples above illustrate, coordinate adjectives differ from serial items in that a comma may be used *without* the coordinating conjunctions *and* or *or* to separate only *two* coordinate adjectives. In regard to comma usage before a first and after a final coordinate adjective, however, the comma rule for coordinate adjectives is the same as the comma rule for serial items.

---

Comma Rule #71: Do not use a comma before a first coordinate adjective or after a last coordinate adjective unless a comma is necessitated by another rule.

## Chapter 9: Common Comma Misuses

- *Incorrect*: The girls dreamed of enjoying another, blue, cloudless day before the end of summer. (The first comma should not be there. No other rule necessitates a comma before the first coordinate adjective.)
- *Correct*: The girls dreamed of enjoying another blue, cloudless day before the end of summer.

- *Correct*: Occurring infrequently this summer, blue, cloudless days are much more appreciated than usual. (In this sentence, the comma before the first coordinate adjective, *blue*, is appropriate because *Occurring infrequently this summer* is a participial phrase, and a comma should follow a participial phrase that begins a sentence. See Comma Rule #16 from chapter 3.)

# Appendix
# List of Comma Rules with Rule Examples

## From Chapter 2: Independent and Dependent Clauses

Comma Rule #1: A sentence comprised of two independent clauses or complete thoughts should be joined by both a comma and a coordinating conjunction, and the comma should be placed immediately after the first clause or complete thought.

- Jerry watched television all night, and Robert went to bed early.
- The Braves won the game, but the Red Sox made fewer errors.
- The bank in his hometown would not accept his check, so Lou was forced to drive ten miles to the nearest ATM machine.

Comma Rule #2: When a sentence contains three or more independent clauses or complete thoughts and two of them function as compound elements that express cause, effect, or contrast in relationship to the other(s), the comma between the like clauses or complete thoughts should usually be omitted, especially if the clauses or complete thoughts are short.

- *Mr. Santana allowed students to catch up on late work* and *Mrs. Lopez showed a film clip,* so *Alex did not have a very demanding day at school.* (The first two clauses function together to express cause.)
- *A lot of rain fell all night,* so *the game was cancelled* and *the other team went home.* (The last two clauses express effect.)

- *The walls are black* and *the carpet is pink*, but *the curtains are red* and *the trim is green*. (The first two clauses contrast "equally" with the last two clauses.)

> Comma Rule #3: When a pair of independent clauses or complete thoughts follows an introductory element that requires a comma, and when the introductory element modifies both clauses, the comma between the two independent clauses should usually be omitted.

- Since you don't know the city very well, you should not talk to strangers and you should not enter any strange buildings. (The dependent clause *Since you don't know the city very well* expresses the reason for the instruction in both of the independent clauses that follow.)
- With much anxiety, Sam returned to his seat and Jill awaited the verdict. (If the prepositional phrase *With much anxiety* is intended to modify both of the independent clauses that follow, then the comma between the independent clauses should be omitted. However, if the prepositional phrase is meant to modify only the first independent clause—*Sam returned to his seat*—then a comma should be used to separate the independent clauses, as in the sentence below.)

    o  With much anxiety, Sam returned to his seat, and Jill awaited the verdict.

> Comma Rule #4: *Generally*, a comma should follow a sentence-beginning dependent clause that begins with a subordinating conjunction and is followed by an independent clause.

- *While he cleaned his room,* he found homework assignments from his seventh-grade year.
- *Since Austin is a long way from Kansas City,* the couple decided to book a flight.

Appendix

> Comma Rule #5: *Generally*, a comma is not necessary after a sentence-beginning independent clause or complete thought that is followed by a dependent clause. However, when an adverbial dependent clause follows an independent clause or complete thought and the dependent clause communicates a contrast, exception, condition, or other sentiment that the writer wishes to emphasize with a pause, a comma may separate the clauses.

- Don't go to the party, since you might get in trouble if you do.
- Jackie played the cello, whereas Ben played the tuba.
- You may come in the house, though you might want to clean your shoes before you do.

> Comma Rule #6: *Generally*, a comma is not necessary after a sentence-beginning independent clause or complete thought that is followed by a dependent clause. However, a comma may be used after an independent clause or complete thought that is followed by a dependent clause when the sentence and the clauses within it are long and a comma would therefore facilitate a natural pause if the sentence were read aloud.

- If a college wants to offer a degree in history with emphasis in teaching licensure, it will need to answer a number of important questions, and it will need to seek formal approval from its accrediting agency and from all internal governing officials, *since a history degree with emphasis in teaching licensure is an entirely different degree.*

> Comma Rule #7: When a pair of dependent clauses begins a sentence and the second clause "completes" the first, a comma should not separate the two clauses. If the second clause functions independently of the first, however, a comma should separate the two clauses.

- <u>Because Rick used a ladder that was old</u>, he had an unfortunate accident.

- <u>Although Ashley is saving a lot of money,</u> <u>unless her wages increase,</u> she will not be able to afford her dream car.

# From Chapter 3: Introductory Elements

---
Comma Rule #8: A comma should follow an adverb that begins a sentence, modifies a verb, and is not followed immediately by the verb it modifies.

---

- *Jubilantly,* he received the championship trophy from the league director.
- *Reluctantly,* she drove to Washington to see her uncle.

---
Comma Rule #9: A comma should follow an adverb that begins a sentence and modifies the rest of the sentence.

---

- *Unfortunately,* seeing the movie was a waste of my time.
- *Apparently,* going to class is a requirement for getting a good grade.

---
Comma Rule #10: A comma *may* follow an adverb of time that begins a sentence.

---

- *Yesterday,* Joey and Ginger went to the retirement home to see their grandfather.
- *Afterwards,* the bartender served free drinks because he was so excited about the victory.
- *Today* he went to the store.
  or
- *Today,* he went to the store.

## Appendix

> Comma Rule #11: A comma should follow a transitional word or expression that begins a sentence.

- *On the one hand*, it is important to stay informed through the media.
- *In the meantime*, he cleaned his room.
- *First*, take the meat from the freezer and defrost it. *Second*, marinate the meat for at least six hours.

> Comma Rule #12: A comma should follow a present or past participle that begins a sentence and is not immediately followed by a dependent clause or a prepositional phrase.

- *Driving*, the man could not answer his cell phone in time.
- *Angered*, Sherry told her children to eat their food or go to their rooms.

> Comma Rule #13: A comma should follow an interjection that begins a sentence and does not require an exclamation point.

- *Oh*, I did not realize I had cut in line.
- *Yes*, the check is in the mail.

> Comma Rule #14: Generally, a comma should follow a prepositional phrase that begins a sentence and is not immediately followed by a dependent clause or a verb. If the subject of the verb is the "understood *you*," however, a comma should be placed between the prepositional phrase and the verb.

- *In the first quarter*, the quarterback completed seven passes.
- *With some hesitation*, Sally agreed to serve as a judge of the students' projects.
- *Under the old maple tree* <u>was</u> a valuable collection of fossils.
- *After the party*, <u>go</u> to the Lankfords' house to pick up your sister.

Appendix

> Comma Rule #15: When consecutive prepositional phrases begin a sentence, a comma should follow the *final* phrase as long as it is not immediately followed by a dependent clause or a verb. If the subject of the verb is the "understood *you*," however, a comma should be placed between the final introductory phrase and the verb.

- <u>*In the middle of the night,*</u> Suzie awoke from a bad dream.
- <u>*Across the Delaware River toward the tavern by Washington's post,*</u> the troops gathered.
- *In the middle of the stream* <u>was</u> a large trout.
- *After the performance at the end of the day,* <u>make</u> sure you clean the equipment.

> Comma Rule #16: A comma should follow a participial phrase that begins a sentence.

- *Questioned about his involvement in the crime,* the man began to worry.
- *Helping whenever she sees an opportunity,* the woman is proving to be a wonderful asset to the firm.

> Comma Rule #17: A comma should follow an infinitive phrase that begins a sentence and functions as an adverb that describes a verb.

- *To win the contest,* you must practice for the next seven weeks. (The infinitive phrase is used as an adverb to describe why you *must practice,* so a comma is placed after the phrase.)
- *To win the contest* is to become the champion. (The infinitive phrase is used as the subject of the sentence—a noun phrase—so no comma is necessary.)

> Comma Rule #18: A comma should follow an absolute phrase that begins a sentence.

- *All things being equal,* the girls have a good shot at winning.

- *Rain pouring down on the roof,* the couple huddled inside by the fireplace during the storm.

# From Chapter 4: Mid-sentence and End-of-sentence Elements

Comma Rule #19: Commas should be placed around a nonrestrictive element that occurs in the middle of a sentence, and a comma should precede a nonrestrictive element that occurs at the end of a sentence.

- Dr. Fuller attended Harvard College, *which has been around for over three hundred years.*
- Carlos married Juanita, *who was born in Canada.*
- Taryn placed her muddy shoes on the couch, *which was purchased at the local furniture store.*

Comma Rule #20: Commas should be placed around a minimally interruptive parenthetical expression that occurs in the middle of a sentence, and a comma should precede a minimally interruptive parenthetical expression that occurs at the end of a sentence.

- The movie's sequel, *according to the local teenagers who recently went to see it,* is not as technologically innovative as the original.
- The Grand Canyon, *some say,* was once used as a giant fortress for Native Americans.
- My brother's new book is not worth the paper it is printed on, *in one critic's opinion.*
- The woman's recovery, *we all hope,* will be a speedy one.

Comma Rule #21: Commas should be placed around a conjunctive adverb or other transitional expression that occurs in the middle of a sentence and *precedes* the main verb, and a comma should precede a conjunctive adverb or other transitional expression that occurs at the end of a sentence.

Appendix

- The mouse fell for the trap. The rat, *however,* <u>was</u> too smart.
- The job's salary would be nice. The long hours, *on the other hand,* <u>are</u> not so desirable.
- Little Bobby hated the grocery store, and his sister, *similarly,* <u>detested</u> the Post Office.
- Professional athletes in the major sports participate in long seasons. Baseball players play from April through September, *for example.*

> Comma Rule #22: Commas may or may not be placed around a mid-sentence conjunctive adverb or other transitional expression that occurs immediately after a verb. In most such cases, the decision to set off the transitional expression with commas—either after a linking verb, helping verb, action verb, or after an entire verb phrase—is a matter of the writer's taste.

- The mouse ingested the poison. It is, *therefore,* dead.
- The mouse ingested the poison. It is *therefore* dead.

> Comma Rule #23: Commas should be placed around a contrasting element that occurs in the middle of a sentence, and a comma should precede a contrasting element that occurs at the end of a sentence.

- Curling, *unlike bowling,* is played on ice.
- The meal was charged to Paul's credit card, *not Barbara's.*

# From Chapter 5: Standard Serial Items and Coordinate Adjectives

> Comma Rule #24: Commas should be used to separate all of the items in a series of like elements, and the coordinating conjunction *and* or *or* should be placed after the comma that separates the last and second-to-last items.

# Appendix

- *Linda, Jerry, and Joseph* attended the matinee together. (three words used as subjects)
- *Allie, Jenny, or Lauren* should clean up the mess. (three words used as subjects)
- Joseph *ran, jogged, walked, and stretched* to prepare for the day's game. (four words used as verbs)
- While he was camping, Brett cooked *hamburgers, potatoes, and steaks*. (three words used as direct objects)
- The *red, green, and gold* chair was almost ruined. (three words used as adjectives)
- Lydia played *by the pool, under the tree, and on the lawn* as she waited for her father. (three adverbial prepositional phrases)
- When Samson's mother returned home, she discovered *that Josie had made a mess on the floor, that Danielle had broken a window, and that Missy had fed the dog too much food*. (three dependent clauses)

---

Comma Rule #25: Commas should separate coordinate adjectives that precede the nouns or pronouns they modify, and the use of the coordinating conjunction *and* or *or* between either a pair of coordinate adjectives or between the last two items in a series of coordinate adjectives is a matter of authorial preference.

---

- Johnson tried to avoid the *smoky, dingy* bar.
- The *rickety, dangerous* elevator frightened all who looked upon it.
- *Windy, slick* roads should be avoided, especially at night.

Appendix

# From Chapter 6: Quotations and Dialogue, Direct Address, and Tag Questions

> Comma Rule #26: When a quotation that ends a sentence follows a phrase such as *according to* or *as [someone] puts it*, or explanatory information containing the word *said* or one of its substitutes, and when the quotation does not blend with the grammatical structure of the sentence, a comma should be placed immediately after the explanatory information that precedes the quotation.

- John *said*, "Get back to your room!"
- After he ate dinner, Uncle Joe relaxed in his chair and *exclaimed*, "That was the best steak I've ever had!"
- Speaking to a large audience, the guest speaker *cautioned*, "We should all stop worrying about things we cannot control."
- The president *declared* in response to the offense, "A new curfew will be imposed across town." (Note that the quotation does not need to start *immediately* after *said* or one of its substitutes. In this sentence, for example, the prepositional phrases *in response* and *to the offense* follow the verb *declared*. When additional explanatory information follows the verb, the comma is placed at the end of the explanatory information.)

> Comma Rule #27: When a quotation begins a sentence and is followed by a phrase such as *according to* or *as [someone] puts it*, or explanatory information containing the word *said* or one of its substitutes, and when the quotation does not blend with the grammatical structure of the sentence, a comma should be placed immediately before the closing quotation marks.

- "We need a bigger house," Suzie said as her sister put away her clothes.
- "I hope it snows tomorrow," Johnny said as he stared with excitement at his new sled.

Appendix

> Comma Rule #28: When a quotation occurs in the middle of a sentence and is either preceded by or followed by a phrase such as *according to* or *as [someone] puts it*, or explanatory information containing the word *said* or one of its substitutes, and when the quotation does not blend with the grammatical structure of the sentence, a comma should be placed immediately after the explanatory information to its left and immediately before its closing quotation marks.

- Ian warned, "Those clouds are moving toward us," but the group was caught in the storm anyway.
- After the game, the coach told his players, "I am very proud of you," and many of the girls cried.
- The rancher said to the farmer, "I've tried everything I know to keep my livestock out of your field," yet the rancher's cows continued to ruin the farmer's corn.

> Comma Rule #29: When a quotation is broken by a phrase such as *according to* or *as [someone] puts it*, or explanatory information containing the word *said* or one of its substitutes, a comma should be placed immediately before the closing quotation marks in the first part of the quotation and immediately after the explanatory information that precedes the second part of the quotation.

- "This restaurant's salsa," said the waiter, "is the best in the city."
- "When summer arrives," declared Melissa, "the beach will be my home."
- "I'm tired," complained the small child to his mother, "but I don't want to go home yet."
- "Get out of my room," the girl shouted to her little brother, "and don't come back!"

> Comma Rule #30: A comma should be placed immediately after direct address that begins a sentence.

- *Friends*, I have some good news.

## Appendix

- *Ladies and gentlemen*, the program will begin in five minutes.
- *Robert, Leroy,* and *Dillon*, please pass your papers to the front of the room.

> Comma Rule #31: Commas should surround direct address that occurs in the middle of a sentence.

- The food, *folks*, is in the refrigerator.
- Your meatloaf, *Mom*, was delicious.

> Comma Rule #32: A comma should precede direct address that ends a sentence.

- Do you know where we are going, *Sherry*?
- How far before we reach the other side, *Bill*?

> Comma Rule #33: A comma should precede a tag question that occurs at the end of a sentence.

- We are not going to the play tonight, *are we*?
- The bill is on the table, *right*?

> Comma Rule #34: Commas should be placed around a tag question that occurs in the middle of a sentence.

- The game will go faster, *won't it*, if we allow only two strikes instead of three?

# From Chapter 7: Dates, Addresses and City/State Locations, Titles and Designations, Numbers, and Correspondence

> Comma Rule #35: In the month-day-year style for writing dates, commas are placed between the calendar day and the year and between the weekday and the month, if a weekday is used.

## Appendix

- Hattie was born on Friday, July 6, 1933.
- The centennial celebration is scheduled for Wednesday, October 15, 2012.
- I have to see the dentist on Monday, June 3.

> Comma Rule #36: When dates written in the month-day-year style occur at the beginning of or in the middle of a sentence, commas should be placed on both sides of the year.

- September 11, 2001, was a sad day for Americans.
- Everyone should return home on Wednesday, October 15, 2012, for the centennial celebration.
- Scott's test date of Thursday, January 14, 2011, has been scheduled for over a year.

> Comma Rule #37: A comma should be placed between a city (or a county) and its state.

- Johnny lives in Salem, Massachusetts.
- Have you even been to Kansas City, Missouri?
- George Viking
  104 South Limestone Road
  Rocky, OK 05555

> Comma Rule #38: When the city (or county) and state are written at the beginning of or in the middle of a sentence, commas should be placed on both sides of the state.

- Kansas City, Missouri, has a great deal of baseball history.
- Please go to the company's headquarters in Salem, Massachusetts, to claim your prize.

> Comma Rule #39: Whether an address is written in block form or in a sentence, a comma should separate (1) a street name from a building name and/or a room number and (2) a personal or company name from a title or designation.

# Appendix

- *Address that contains both a building name and a room number:*
  Capstone Toys
  9241 Flint Boulevard, Suite 4C
  Firehouse, IN 05555

- *Address that contains both a title and a designation:*
  Cabin Products, Inc.
  Attention: Paul Krauss, Ph.D.
  Pinewood, NY 05555
  (Commas with titles and designations will be addressed in more detail with Comma Rule #41.)

---

Comma Rule #40: When addresses are written in a sentence, commas should be used where line breaks would be used if the address were written in block form, and any commas required within a line in block form should be retained.

---

- Please mail the package to Jill Nichols, 401 Washington Street, Tacoma, Washington 05555.
- My grandmother's address is 23 North Pike Avenue, Apartment 7, High Mountain, South Dakota 05555.

---

Comma Rule #41: A comma should precede a title or designation that is used after a personal or company name at the end of a sentence or address line, and commas should be placed on both sides of a title or designation that is used in the middle of a sentence or mailing line.

---

- John Roberts, M.D.
- Please call Hearty Auto Sales, Inc.
- Diane Stevens, D.D., is the best dentist I know.
- Marty Greenboro, Director of Human Relations, will speak to all employees on Monday.

## Appendix

> **Comma Rule #42:** Unless a number represents a zip code, a street address, a four-digit year, or a page number, commas should be placed to the left of every third digit in numbers that contain four or more digits.

- 1,298 turtles
- 101,456 towns in cities
- $488,297,444
- 1,333,087,412 trees

> **Comma Rule #43:** Commas should be used to separate measurements, parts, or categories that communicate a difference in size, space, or scope.

- act III, scene 3
- six feet, seven inches
- chapter 4, part 1
- page 9, line 6
- row 11, seat 23

> **Comma Rule #44:** Commas should follow salutations (greetings) in informal correspondence and closings in all correspondence.

- Salutations:  Dear Ms. Knight,
  Greetings,
  Professor Kensington,

- Closings:  Sincerely,
  Yours truly,
  Best wishes,
  Respectfully,

Appendix

# From Chapter 8: Difficult Cases and Rules Less Frequently Needed

> Comma Rule #45: When commas are used within serial items, semicolons instead of commas should separate the items themselves.

- Jerry, who is British, plays soccer; Jordan, who is American, plays baseball; and James, who is Canadian, plays polo.
- The candidates were Margaret Whitmore, age 18; Sandy Jansen, age 19; and Molly Flickner, age 19.
- The tour consisted of stops in Kalamazoo, Michigan; Springfield, Missouri; and Chicago.

> Comma Rule #46: When parentheses enclose numbers used to designate serial items in a sentence, an opening parenthesis should be treated as the first word of each serial item.

- When you heat the microwave pizza, remember to (1) remove the pizza from the box, (2) remove the plastic wrapping from the pizza, and (3) select the proper cooking time from the microwave's control panel.
- Margaret told her oldest son to (1) take out the trash, (2) wash the dishes, (3) clean his room, and (4) change the oil in the car.

> Comma Rule #47: When text within parentheses interrupts the usual placement of a comma, the comma should be placed immediately after the closing parenthesis.

- Nadia's painting was beautiful (she worked on it for months), and her sculpture wasn't bad, either. (The comma is needed to separate the two independent clauses that are joined by the coordinating conjunction *and*.)
- Along the riverbank (which is teeming with insects), George is teaching his two youngest children how to fish. (The comma is needed to follow the introductory prepositional phrase.)

## Appendix

- Enjoying the show (the comedian on television was quite funny), Joel forgot about the food that was in the oven. (The comma is needed to follow the introductory participial phrase.)

> Comma Rule #48: Use a comma to separate "the more…the greater…" type sentence elements unless the elements are very short.

- The more you study for your test, the better your grade will be in the class.
- The fewer people who care about participating in the democratic process, the more the government will decide things for us.
- The bigger they are, the harder they fall.
but
- The bigger the better.

> Comma Rule #49: When internal monologue that ends a sentence follows explanatory information containing the word *thought* or one of its substitutes, and when the internal monologue does not blend with the grammatical structure of the sentence, a comma should be placed immediately after the explanatory information that precedes the quotation.

- John thought to himself, *I wish she would leave me alone.*
- After he ate dinner, Uncle Joe relaxed in his chair and thought to himself, *I wonder if Aunt Irene knows how bad that ham is.*
- Staring at a large audience, the guest speaker wondered, *Will they love me or hate me?*

> Comma Rule #50: When internal monologue begins a sentence and is followed by explanatory information containing the word *thought* or one of its substitutes, a comma should be placed immediately after the internal monologue.

- *We need a bigger house,* Suzie thought as she put away her clothes.

- *Please send us some rain,* George prayed silently.

> Comma Rule #51: When internal monologue occurs in the middle of a sentence and is either preceded by or followed by explanatory information containing the word *thought* or one of its substitutes, and when the internal monologue does not blend with the grammatical structure of the sentence, a comma should be placed immediately after the explanatory information to its left and immediately after the end of the monologue, unless the end of the monologue requires a question mark or an exclamation point.

- Ian thought, *Those clouds are moving toward us,* but he did not seek shelter.
- After the game, the coach thought to himself, *I am very proud of my players,* but he did not share the thought with the team.

> Comma Rule #52: When internal monologue is divided by explanatory information, a comma should be placed immediately after the first part of the monologue, immediately before the second part, and immediately after the second part if the second part does not end the sentence.

- *This restaurant's salsa,* thought the customer, *is the best in the city.*
- *When summer arrives,* Melissa mentally noted, *the beach will be my home.*
- *I'm tired,* thought Tina, *but I don't want to go home yet.*

> Comma Rule #53: A question referenced within a sentence should be preceded by a comma.

- The question, where did I place my keys? is one that I ask often.
- Everyone wanted to know the answer to the question, how did the magician do that?

Appendix

> Comma Rule #54: When each element of a "not only...but also..." sentence construction contains both a subject and a verb, a comma should separate the clauses.

- <u>Pam</u> not only <u>grows</u> prize tomatoes, but <u>she</u> also <u>wins</u> blue ribbons for her pumpkins.
- My <u>uncle</u> not only <u>fought</u> bravely in the World War II, <u>he</u> also <u>stopped</u> a bank robbery one time in Tampa, Florida.

> Comma Rule #55: When the elements of a "not only...but also..." sentence construction do not contain both a subject and a verb, a comma should not be used to separate the elements unless the text between "not only" and "but also" phrases is long and the meeting place of the two phrases would necessitate a natural pause if the sentence were read aloud.

- Jason played the game not only with skill but also with poise. (In this sentence, *not only* and *but also* introduce prepositional phrases. The elements lack a subject and verb.)
- Juliet taught her children to be wise not only in choosing their friends and social activities, but also in interacting with people both at work and at play. (*Not only* and *but also* introduce prepositional phrases. Neither element contains both a subject and a verb, but the comma after *activities* may help make the sentence easier to read since a reader would likely pause for a short breath after the word *activities*.)

> Comma Rule #56: To facilitate understanding and easier reading, a comma may separate homonyms that appear beside each other in a sentence, except in sentences involving "that/that" constructions.

- He walked in, in blue jeans.
- The one plant that grew, grew large.

> Comma Rule #57: Commas may be used in the place of words omitted from serial items.

## Appendix

- For Christmas I hope we go to Grandpa Smith's house; for Thanksgiving, Aunt Josie's; and for Memorial Day, Uncle Phil's.
- The Tigers defeated the Red Sox 5–4; the Rangers, 7–2; and the Yankees, 9–0.

> Comma Rule #58: When two introductory elements begin a sentence, a comma should be placed after the first element, but the pause principle and authorial preference should govern the use of a comma after the second element, unless the second element is a transitional expression or a very long element that would naturally necessitate a breathing pause if the sentence were spoken—then a comma should be used.

- <u>Of course, if Hannah leaves a day early</u> she will also be able to
- <u>However, in the winter</u> the drive will be more difficult.
- Matthew does not sleep well when just the fan is going. <u>When the air conditioner is on, however,</u> he sleeps like a baby.
- <u>Yes, when the ice cream truck makes it way from the elementary school to the neighbor's house across the street</u>, you may buy a chocolate sundae.

# From Chapter 9: Common Comma Misuses

> Comma Rule #59: Do not use *only* a comma to join two independent clauses or complete thoughts—a coordinating conjunction must accompany the comma.

- *Incorrect*: Sophia took a walk in the park, Mr. Garcia took his children with him to the supermarket.
- *Correct*: Sophia took a walk in the park<u>, and</u> Mr. Garcia took his children with him to the supermarket.

> Comma Rule #60: Do not use a comma between only two like elements unless a comma is necessitated by another rule.

## Appendix

- *Incorrect:* Linda, and *Jerry* attended the matinee together. (two words used as subjects)
- *Correct:* Linda and *Jerry* attended the matinee together.

- *Incorrect*: Joseph *ran,* and *stretched* to prepare for the day's game. (two words used as verbs)
- *Correct*: Joseph *ran* and *stretched* to prepare for the day's game.

- *Incorrect*: While he was camping, Brett cooked *hamburgers,* and *steaks*. (two words used as direct objects)
- *Correct*: While he was camping, Brett cooked *hamburgers* and *steaks*.

The majority of mistakes related to this issue revolve around misusing a comma with two *verb phrases*. Mistakes such as the one in the sentence below are common.

- *Incorrect*: In an effort to gain national recognition, <u>the college added a number of new academic majors</u>, and <u>expanded its budget for its honors program</u>.
- *Correct*: In an effort to gain national recognition, the college added a number of new academic majors and expanded its budget for its honors program. (No comma is needed after *majors* because the sentence simply contains two verb phrases—*added a number of new academic majors* and *expanded its budget for its honors program*—for the same subject, *college*.)
- *Correct*: In an effort to gain national recognition, the college added a number of new academic majors, and **it** expanded its budget for its honors program. (In this sentence, the word *it* has been added. Now, since *it* functions as the subject of an independent clause, the coordinating conjunction *and* separates two independent clauses. Comma Rule #1 from chapter 2 is therefore applicable: "A sentence comprised of two independent clauses or complete thoughts should be joined by both a comma and a coordinating conjunction, and the comma should be placed immediately after the first clause or complete

thought." Without the word *it*, the sentence simply contains two verb phrases that have the same subject: *college*.)

---

Comma Rule #61: Do not use a comma immediately after a subordinating conjunction unless a comma is necessitated by another rule.

---

- *Incorrect*: Although, I cleaned my room on Saturday morning, I forgot to make my bed.
- *Correct*: Although I cleaned my room on Saturday evening, I forgot to make my bed.

---

Comma Rule #62: Do not use a comma when writing only the month and day or month and year.

---

- *Incorrect*: She lost her purse on July, 20.
- *Correct*: She lost her purse on July 20.
- *Incorrect*: He dropped his wallet in the lake in September, 2003.
- *Correct*: He dropped his wallet in the lake in September 2003.

---

Comma Rule #63: Do not use a comma between a season and a year or between the name of a specific holiday and year.

---

- *Incorrect*: Summer, 1993 was an unforgettable time.
- *Correct*: Summer 1993 was an unforgettable time.

- *Incorrect*: My dad tricked me on Halloween, 1999.
- *Correct*: My dad tricked me on Halloween 1999.

- *Incorrect*: You should go finish your homework unless, you want to be in trouble.
- *Correct*: You should go finish your homework unless you want to be in trouble.

---

Comma Rule #64: Do not use a comma with restrictive family titles such as *Jr., Sr., II, III*, etc.

## Appendix

- *Incorrect*: The package should be addressed to Michael Willowby, III.
- *Correct*: The package should be addressed to Michael Willowby III.

- *Incorrect*: Victor Barron, Jr., is a film director in California.
- *Correct*: Victor Barron Jr. is a film director in California.

Comma Rule #65: Do not use a comma between a subject and its verb(s) unless a comma is necessitated by another rule.

- *Incorrect*: The secretary's <u>report, indicated</u> that too much money was spent on party supplies last year. (The comma is unnecessary in this sentence.)
- *Correct*: The secretary's <u>report</u> <u>indicated</u> that too much money was spent on party supplies last year.

Comma Rule #66: Do not use a comma between an action verb and its object(s) unless a comma is necessitated by another rule.

- *Incorrect*: The thief stole, the couple's new television. (The comma is unnecessary in this sentence.)
- *Correct*: The thief stole the couple's new television.

Comma Rule #67: Do not use a comma between a linking verb and its predicate complement(s) unless a comma is necessitated by another rule.

- *Incorrect*: The speaker is, silly. (The comma is unnecessary in this sentence.)
- *Correct*: The speaker is silly.

Comma Rule #68: Do not use a comma between a preposition and its object(s) unless a comma is necessitated by another rule.

- *Incorrect*: After we arrived at the beach house, we took a nice walk along, the shore. (The second comma is unnecessary.)

# Appendix

- *Correct*: After we arrived at the beach house, we took a nice long walk along the shore.

> Comma Rule #69: Do not use a comma between a major sentence element such as a subject, verb, or complement and a prepositional phrase unless a comma is necessitated by another rule.

- *Incorrect*: Cowboys, on horses are seen often in Pasture County, Montana. (The subject *cowboys* is followed immediately by the prepositional phrase *on horses*. The comma between these two elements should not be there.)
- *Correct*: Cowboys on horses are often seen in Pasture County, Montana.

> Comma Rule #70: Do not use a comma before the first item or after the last item in a series unless a comma is necessitated by another rule.

- *Incorrect*: I spend most of my spare time, *reading, writing,* and *studying*. (The first comma should not be there. No other rule necessitates a comma before the first item in the series.)
- *Correct*: I spend most of my spare time *reading, writing, and studying*.

> Comma Rule #71: Do not use a comma before a first coordinate adjective or after a last coordinate adjective unless a comma is necessitated by another rule.

- *Incorrect*: The girls dreamed of enjoying another, blue, cloudless day before the end of summer. (The first comma should not be there. No other rule necessitates a comma before the first coordinate adjective.)
- *Correct*: The girls dreamed of enjoying another blue, cloudless day before the end of summer.

# Index

**absolute phrase**, 59, 136
**addresses**, 91, 92, 93, 94, 121, 143, 144
**adjectives**, 3, 7, 8, 9, 10, 12, 13, 14, 15, 19, 26, 27, 28, 41, 42, 46, 47, 48, 53, 54, 55, 61, 64, 71, 72, 73, 74, 75, 76, 97, 104, 117, 118, 124, 125, 129, 130, 138, 139, 154
    *a, an, the* as, 8
    clause, 26, 28, 29, 31, 60
    coordinate, 71, 73, 74, 75, 129, 130, 138, 139, 154
    commas and, 74, 138, 139
    comma misuse with, 129, 154
    defined, 7
    in prepositional phrases, 12, 13, 125
    other parts of speech functioning as, 8, 75-76
    prepositional phrases as, 12, 13
    proper, 104
    *See also* participle; participial phrase
**antecedent**, 6, 7
    defined, 5
**articles**
    defined, 8
    definite, 8
    indefinite, 8

**adverb**, 9, 10, 11, 12, 13, 14, 15, 26, 27, 28, 31, 35, 38, 41, 42, 43, 44, 46, 55, 56, 59, 66, 67, 71, 72, 76, 98, 112, 117, 118, 133, 134, 136, 137, 138, 139
    clause, 26, 27, 31
    conjunctive (*see also* transitional expression), 11, 46, 59, 66, 67, 112, 137, 138
    defined, 9
**appositive**, 63, 64, 73

**capitalization**, 3, 80, 81, 85, 102, 104, 105, 106
**clause**
    adverb, 26, 27, 31
    adjective, 26, 28, 29, 31, 60
    defined, 23
    dependent, 6, 14, 23, 24, 25, 26, 27, 28, 29, 30, 31, 35, 36, 37, 38, 39, 40, 48, 50, 51, 52, 53, 55, 56, 71, 72, 80, 81, 84, 98, 111, 112, 113, 117, 120, 127, 132, 135, 136, 139
    defined, 25
    independent, 23, 24, 25, 26, 27, 29, 30, 31, 32, 33, 34, 35, 36, 37, 38, 39, 40, 42, 68, 81, 84, 100, 101, 115, 116, 118, 119, 128, 129, 131, 132, 133, 146, 150, 151
    defined, 25

# Index

noun, 26, 30, 37, 80
subordinate (*see also* dependent clause), 25, 26
**colon**, 96
**comma splice**, 32, 115
**compound elements**, 7, 17, 20, 34, 131
    comma misuse with, 117, 118, 119
**conjunction**, 11
    coordinating, 30, 31, 32, 33, 35, 50, 68, 72, 73, 74, 84, 97, 100, 104, 115, 116, 119, 128, 129, 131, 138, 139, 146, 150, 151
    list of, 14, 31
    omission of with
        coordinate adjectives, 74, 129, 139
    with comma and
        independent clauses, 30, 31, 32, 68, 84, 115, 119, 129, 146, 150, 151
    with comma and serial
        items, 33, 72, 97, 99, 117, 129, 138
    correlative, 14, 15, 26
    defined, 14
    subordinating, 14, 26, 27, 28, 36, 37, 68, 69, 132
        comma misuse with, 120, 152
        *however* used as, 68–69
        list of, 27
        with comma and sentence-beginning dependent clauses, 36, 81, 132
**contrasting elements**, 59, 69, 126, 127, 128
**correspondence**, 89, 96, 145
    closings, 96, 145
    salutations, 96, 145

**dates**, 89, 90, 120, 121, 142, 143
    comma misuse with, 120, 121
    day-month-year style, 90–91
    month-day-year style, 89, 90, 142, 143
**dependent clause**, 6, 14, 23, 24, 25, 26, 27, 28, 29, 30, 31, 35, 36, 37, 38, 39, 40, 48, 50, 51, 52, 53, 55, 56, 71, 72, 80, 81, 84, 98, 111, 112, 113, 117, 120, 127, 132, 135, 136, 139
    defined, 25
**dialogue** (*see also* quotations), 77, 101, 102, 140
**direct address**, 77, 85, 86, 141, 142
**direct object(s)**, 19, 20, 30, 71, 72, 80, 97, 108, 117, 118, 123, 127, 128, 139, 151

**exclamation point**, 15, 48, 49, 82, 83, 103, 104, 135, 148

**family titles**, 121, 122, 152

**gerund**, 47, 54

**holidays**, 120, 121, 152
**homonyms that appear beside each other**, 108, 109, 149

# Index

104, 106, 148
**questions referenced as questions**, 106, 107, 148
**quotation marks**, 77, 80, 82, 83, 84, 85, 101, 102, 140, 141
**quotations**, 77–85, 102, 140
    use of *that* with, 79–80
**restrictive elements**, 38, 60, 61, 64, 122, 152
**run-on sentence**, 32

**seasons**, 120, 121, 152
**semicolon**, 30, 68, 98, 99, 116, 146
**series/serial items**, 32, 33, 71, 72, 73, 74, 97, 98, 99, 109, 110, 117, 118, 128, 129, 138, 139, 146, 149, 154
**subject(s)**, 16, 17, 18, 19, 23, 24, 25, 26, 27, 28, 29, 30, 31, 36, 37, 41, 47, 49, 50, 51, 52, 53, 54, 55, 56, 57, 67, 68, 71, 72, 84, 97, 107, 108, 111, 117, 118, 119, 122, 123, 124, 125, 126, 127, 135, 136, 139, 149, 151, 152, 153, 154
    simple, 16, 17, 19
    understood *you* as, 18, 50, 51, 52, 53, 135, 136
**subordinate clause** (see also *dependent clause*), 25, 26

**tag questions**, 77, 86, 87, 140, 142
*the more, the better, the greater* **and similar expressions**, 100, 147
*that* vs. *which*, 60
**titles and designations**, 89, 93, 94, 122, 142, 144

family titles, 121, 122, 152
**transitional expression**, 11, 44, 45, 46, 59, 66, 67, 68, 69, 111, 112, 137, 138, 150
    list of, 45
**transitive verb(s)**, 19, 20

**understood** *you*, 18, 50, 51, 52, 53, 133, 136

**verb**
    action, 3, 4, 5, 16, 17, 19, 20, 67, 68, 123, 124, 138, 153
    defined, 3
    helping, 3, 4, 5, 17, 46, 48, 53, 61, 62, 67, 68, 138
    linking, 3, 4, 5, 7, 19, 67, 124, 125, 138, 153
    transitive, 19, 20

*which* vs. *that*, 60
*who* vs. *which/that*, 63

www.ingramcontent.com/pod-product-compliance
Lightning Source LLC
Chambersburg PA
CBHW052341230426
43664CB00041B/2604